THE RICHEST MAN IN BABYLON – FOR EVERYONE

GEORGE S. CLASON

Edited by
RICHARD ENLOW

FOR EVERYONE BOOKS

For Spencer—my partner, my inspiration, and the one who helped me start my own financial journey. Your encouragement has meant everything.

A NOTE ON THE TEXT & THIS ADAPTATION

This book is a simplified version of *The Richest Man in Babylon*. The original text, written by George S. Clason in 1926, shares timeless financial wisdom through parables set in ancient Babylon. While the lessons remain valuable, the language and storytelling style can feel outdated or overly formal to modern readers.

This adaptation preserves the core principles of the original—saving, investing, and building wealth—but presents them in a clearer, more accessible way. The goal is to make these financial lessons easy to understand and apply, so that anyone can use them to build a more secure and prosperous future.

FOREWORD

Money influences every part of our lives, yet most of us are never taught how to manage it effectively. When I first read The Richest Man in Babylon, I was amazed by its wisdom. But the old-fashioned language made it tough for modern readers to understand. I made this adaptation to clarify important financial lessons. I want them to be more accessible and easier to apply today.

The Richest Man in Babylon was written almost a hundred years ago. It still stands as one of the best financial guides ever published. The principles of saving, investing, living within your means, and making smart choices matter just as much today as they did long ago. The only thing that needed updating was the way they were told.

This book focuses on financial success. It's not about luck. Instead, it emphasizes knowledge, discipline, and smart choices. George S. Clason wrote *The Richest Man in Babylon* to empower people to take control of their financial future. His message was clear: nations thrive when their people do. Similarly, individuals succeed by managing their money wisely.

Wealth isn't built by chance; it's created through consistent effort and smart financial habits. The Babylonians had no natural riches, yet they became the wealthiest of their time. They did this by following simple money principles that still work today.

This adaptation preserves Clason's wisdom while making it easier to understand and put into action. No matter if you want to pay off debt, save money, or plan for the future, these lessons will guide you to success.

I think everyone should have access to financial education. It shouldn't depend on their background or experience. No matter where you're starting from, wealth is built one smart decision at a time. I hope this book helps you take that first step.

— *Richard Enlow*

1

A BRIEF HISTORY OF BABYLON

The Rise and Rule of Babylon

Few cities in history are as legendary as Babylon. Its very name conjures images of wealth, power, and splendor. The city had gold, jewels, and tall buildings that were priceless. It was one of the greatest wonders of the ancient world. But its success was not due to abundant natural resources. In fact, Babylon had almost none.

Babylon didn't grow in fertile valleys or near trade routes. Instead, it emerged from dry, flat land next to the Euphrates River. It had no forests for timber, no mines for precious metals, and not even stones for building. Rainfall was scarce, making agriculture difficult. At first glance, it seemed an unlikely place for a great civilization to emerge.

Yet, Babylon flourished—not by chance, but by the ingenuity and determination of its people.

The Babylonians had two natural advantages: fertile soil and river water. They didn't accept the limits of their land. Their engineers created a smart irrigation system. They used large canals and dams to move water. This change turned a dry area into a top agricultural center in the ancient world. This system was so sophisticated that its impact can still be seen today.

Babylon didn't rely on conquest like many empires. Its power grew from wisdom, strong leadership, and innovation. The rulers had to protect their land from invaders who wanted its wealth. However, they cared more about wise governance than about expanding through war. Rather than seeking to conquer distant lands, they built wealth through knowledge, trade, and progress.

But even the greatest cities do not last forever.

As the energy and ambition that built Babylon faded, so too did the city itself. Over time, its people abandoned it, leaving its grand structures to crumble into dust. What was once the wealthiest city on Earth became nothing more than scattered ruins.

Today, Babylon's remains lie in modern-day Iraq, about 600 miles east of the Suez Canal, near the Persian Gulf. Its latitude aligns with Yuma, Arizona, and it shares a similarly harsh, unforgiving climate. Where a bustling city once thrived, only desert remains. Small nomadic tribes now struggle to survive off the land.

For centuries, travelers mistook Babylon's ruins for nothing more than rolling hills of earth. Archaeologists found pottery and brick fragments. Then they realized these "hills" were buried cities, hidden under years of sand and dust. Excavations funded by Europe and America found the remains of this great civilization. They remind us that even the wealthiest cities can't escape time.

Babylon was once a symbol of success. Now, it teaches us a lesson: wealth and power can rise, but without vision and effort, even the greatest empires will fall.

Babylon's Legacy

Historians think Babylon is one of the oldest civilizations. Its written records go back at least 8,000 years. Astronomers verified this by looking at descriptions of an ancient solar eclipse in Babylonian texts. They calculated when the eclipse was visible in Babylon. This helped them connect Babylonian dates to our modern calendar.

The Babylonians were pioneers in many fields. They were the first in engineering, astronomy, mathematics, and finance. Their irrigation canals—some wide enough for twelve horses to ride side by side—turned the desert into farmland. They also drained swamps near the rivers to create even more fertile land.

The Greek historian Herodotus, who visited Babylon in its prime, described the city in great detail. He marveled at its wealth, vast fields of wheat and barley, and the cleverness of its people.

The Babylonians used clay tablets instead of paper. They baked the tablets to make them hard, so they wouldn't decay over time. Thousands of tablets have been found. They reveal insights into daily life, trade, owning property, and personal letters. One tablet shows a trade. A man exchanged a cow for seven sacks of wheat. He received three sacks right away, and he will get the rest later.

The Great Walls of Babylon

One of Babylon's most famous wonders was its massive walls. Ancient writers ranked them alongside the Great Pyramid of Egypt as one of the "Seven Wonders of the World."

Queen Semiramis built the first walls. However, the most impressive ones came later. Around 600 BC, King Nabopolassar and his son Nebuchadnezzar built them. Nebuchadnezzar is also known from the Bible. These walls were a stunning feat of engineering. They stood about 160 feet high, equal to a 15-story building. They stretched around the city for 9 to 11 miles. The top was so wide that a six-horse chariot could ride along it. Today, little remains of these walls except parts of the foundation and the moat. Over time, the Arabs repurposed the bricks for other buildings, erasing much of Babylon's former grandeur.

Babylon had strong defenses, but it fell not by force. Instead, it fell through strategy. Around 540 BC, the Persian king Cyrus set out to conquer the city. He didn't attack the huge walls. Instead, he tricked King Nabonidus of Babylon into sending his army out to battle. After defeating them in open battle, Cyrus walked into the city unchallenged. This marked the beginning of Babylon's decline, and within a few centuries, it was completely abandoned.

The Lasting Influence of Babylon

Babylon may be gone, but its influence still affects the world today. The Babylonians were pioneers in finance and trade. They invented money for trade. They also created promissory notes and wrote property records. They also did well in crafts like metalwork, weaving, jewelry-making, and sculpture.

While many people used stone tools, the Babylonians had metal weapons and farming gear. Their progress in astronomy and math built the base for future civilizations.

The wisdom of Babylon has survived, even as its walls have crumbled. Its teachings on money and success remain just as true today as they were thousands of years ago.

The Timeless Laws of Wealth

• Money is the measure of success in the physical world.

• Money makes it possible to enjoy the best that life has to offer.

• Money is plentiful for those who understand the simple rules of acquiring it.

• Money is still controlled by the same principles that governed it when Babylon was the wealthiest city on Earth, 6,000 years ago.

The riches of Babylon may have faded into history, but the financial wisdom of its people endures. Those who follow these timeless laws can still build their own wealth today, just as the Babylonians did long ago.

Key Takeaways

1 **Wealth Comes from Wisdom, Not Luck.** Babylon thrived without natural riches. Its success came from hard work, smart planning, and financial wisdom.

2 **Smart Planning Creates Opportunity.** The Babylonians turned their tough surroundings into a busy city. They did this with engineering, trade, and smart planning.

3 **Financial Principles Never Change.** The same money rules that made Babylon wealthy—saving, investing, and wise spending—still apply today.

4 **Security Protects Wealth.** Babylon's strong walls kept its wealth safe. In the same way, today's financial security—like savings, investments, and knowledge—helps protect our wealth.

5 **Success is Earned, Not Given.** The Babylonians thrived because they put in the effort. This shows that anyone can create wealth with discipline and determination.

2

THE MAN WHO WANTED GOLD

A Troubled Craftsman

Bansir, a chariot builder in Babylon, sat on the low wall by his home. He gazed at his small house and the unfinished chariot in his workshop. His wife peeked out from the doorway now and then, silently reminding him that their food supply was running low. He should have been working—hammering, carving, and stretching leather over the wheel rims. But instead, he sat there, lost in thought.

The scorching Babylonian sun beat down on him, making sweat drip from his forehead, but he didn't notice. His mind was struggling with a problem, one that had no easy answer.

Around him, the grand city of Babylon buzzed with life. Just beyond his home, the towering walls of the king's palace loomed high. The beautifully painted Temple of Bel stretched toward the sky. The streets bustled with the rich in grand chariots, traders in sandals, and beggars with bare feet. Even the rich had to move aside for the long line of slaves. They carried heavy goatskins filled with water for the king's famous hanging gardens.

Bansir didn't pay attention to the noisy streets. He was too deep in his thoughts—until he heard the familiar sound of a lyre being played. He turned to see his best friend, Kobbi, the musician, smiling at him.

A Friend's Request

"May the gods bless you with great fortune, my friend," Kobbi said, giving an exaggerated bow. "It seems they already have, since you're relaxing instead of working. I'd love to share in your good fortune. Lend me two shekels until after the noblemen's feast tonight. You won't even miss them before I pay you back."

Bansir sighed heavily. "If I had two shekels, I wouldn't lend them to anyone—not even you, my best friend. Because those two shekels would be my entire fortune. And no man lends away his entire fortune."

Kobbi's eyes widened in shock. "You don't have even one shekel? And yet, here you sit like a statue! Why aren't you working on that chariot? How else will you afford to eat? This isn't like you. What's wrong? Has bad luck struck you?"

A Dream of Wealth

"It must be a curse from the gods," Bansir admitted. "It all started with a dream—a foolish dream. In it, I was a wealthy man. My belt held a heavy purse filled with coins. I tossed silver to beggars, bought fine clothes for my wife, and had gold to spare, making me feel safe and unafraid of the future. I was content. My wife was happy, her face free of worry. It was a beautiful dream."

Kobbi laughed. "A pleasant dream indeed. But why let it turn you into a lifeless statue?"

"Because when I woke up and saw my empty purse, a terrible feeling came over me. I realized that we have been working hard all our lives, yet we remain poor. We live in the richest city in the world, surrounded by gold and wealth. And yet, here we are—struggling to get by. Why? Why do we earn so much but have nothing to show for it?"

Kobbi's smile faded. "I don't know the answer. I work hard, too, but my coins disappear as quickly as I earn them. I barely manage to keep my family fed. And in my heart, I long for a grand lyre—one that could produce music more beautiful than even the king has ever heard."

Bansir nodded. "You should have that lyre, Kobbi. No one could play it better than you. But how can we afford such things when we are no better off than the king's slaves?"

Realizing Their Own Poverty

A line of half-naked, sweating water carriers walked up the street. Each man carried a heavy goatskin of water on his back.

"A fine-looking leader they have," Kobbi said, pointing at the man at the front, who carried no load. "He must have been important in his own land."

"There are many strong men in that line," Bansir said, watching them. "Some are tall and blond from the north. Others are dark-skinned from the south. Some are small and brown from nearby lands. All are marching back and forth from the river to the gardens, day after day, year after year. No future. No hope. Just endless labor."

Kobbi sighed. "I pity them. But you make me realize—we are not much better off. We may be free men, but we work just as hard for just as little."

"That's the truth," Bansir agreed. "And I don't want to keep living like this—working endlessly and going nowhere."

"Maybe we could learn from those who have found success," Kobbi suggested.

Bansir's eyes lit up. "Yes! Perhaps there's a secret to wealth that we've never been taught."

A Plan to Seek Wisdom

"This very day," Kobbi said, "I saw our old friend Arkad riding in his golden chariot. He didn't ignore me as others of his wealth might have. Instead, he waved and smiled, greeting me as a friend."

"He is the richest man in Babylon," Bansir mused.

"So rich that even the king seeks his advice on matters of the treasury," Kobbi added.

Bansir chuckled. "So rich that if I met him in the dark, I'd be tempted to steal his heavy purse!"

Kobbi shook his head. "That wouldn't make you rich. A fat purse is useless if it isn't constantly refilled. Arkad has an income—a steady flow of gold that keeps his purse full no matter how much he spends."

"Income!" Bansir exclaimed. "That's what we need! An income that keeps flowing, whether I'm working or resting. Arkad must know how a man can create such wealth. Do you think he could teach us?"

"He must know the answer," Kobbi said. "Didn't he teach his son, Nomasir? The stories say that Nomasir left Babylon with nothing but his father's wisdom, yet he became one of the richest men in Nineveh."

The Journey to Arkad

Bansir's face lit up with determination. "It costs nothing to ask a wise friend for advice. Arkad has always been kind. Let's go to him! Let's ask how we, too, can build wealth and secure an income for ourselves."

Kobbi nodded eagerly. "Yes! We have never truly sought wealth before. We worked hard at our trades—me with my music, you with your chariots—but we never sought the knowledge of how to grow rich. Now, we see the truth: if we want to prosper, we must learn how. With this new understanding, we will find a way to achieve our desires."

"Then let's not waste time," Bansir said. "Let's go to Arkad today. And let's bring others with us—our friends who have struggled just as we have. They, too, should hear his wisdom."

"You've always had a generous heart, Bansir," Kobbi said. "That's why you have so many friends. Let's go, and let's bring them with us!"

Five Key Takeaways

1 **Hard Work Alone Does Not Guarantee Wealth.** – Bansir and Kobbi realize that despite years of effort in their trades, they remain poor. Simply working hard is not enough—understanding how to manage and grow money is essential.

2 **The Rich Think Differently About Money.** Bansir envies Arkad, the richest man in Babylon. But Kobbi reminds him that true wealth isn't just a full purse. It's about having a steady income that keeps it full.

3 **Ignorance About Wealth Keeps People Poor.** – Both men admit they have never truly sought financial knowledge. They now understand that wealth is not about luck but about learning the principles of prosperity.

4 **The Desire for More is the First Step Toward Wealth.** – Bansir's frustration with his situation sparks a new deter-

mination to find answers. Recognizing the need for change is what pushes people toward financial success.

5 Seek Wisdom from Those Who Have Succeeded. – Instead of remaining in ignorance, Bansir and Kobbi decide to learn from Arkad. Having smart mentors is crucial for building wealth.

3

THE RICHEST MAN IN BABYLON

A Question from Old Friends

In ancient Babylon, there once lived a very wealthy man named Arkad. He was famous not only for his great riches but also for his generosity. He gave freely to charity, took care of his family, and spent well on himself. Yet, despite all this, his fortune continued to grow year after year.

Some of his childhood friends came to him one day and said:

"Arkad, you are far richer than we are. While we struggle just to get by, you have become the richest man in Babylon. You wear the best clothes and eat great food. We can hardly afford to dress our families and put food on the table."

"Yet, once we were equals. We studied under the same teachers. We played the same games as children. And you were neither smarter nor more skilled than we were. In all the years since, you have been no more honest or hard-working than us, as far as we can tell."

"So why has fate chosen you for wealth and left us to struggle? Why do you get to enjoy the good things in life while we cannot?"

Wealth Is Not About Luck

Arkad listened to his friends and then replied:

"If you've only had a bare existence, it's likely because you didn't learn the rules of building wealth or you haven't followed them.""

"Luck is an unreliable goddess who brings no lasting success. In fact, she often ruins the men she showers with unearned gold. Some waste everything on silly pleasures. Soon, they feel poorer than before. They can't satisfy their new, costly tastes. Others hoard their gold in fear of losing it, living joyless lives filled with worry.

"Only a rare few can handle sudden wealth wisely, and I have heard of them only in stories. Think of the men you know who have inherited wealth—how many of them have kept and grown it?"

His friends admitted that those who had inherited great fortunes often lost them. So they asked Arkad to explain how he had built his wealth.

The Desire for Wealth

"When I was young," Arkad said, "I looked around and saw all the good things that bring happiness and comfort. I realized that wealth allows people to enjoy more of these things."

"Wealth is power. With it, a man can:"
- Decorate his home with the finest furnishings.
- Travel to distant lands.
- Enjoy exotic foods and wines.
- Buy jewelry and luxurious clothing.
- Build temples to honor the gods.
- And experience many other pleasures that make life enjoyable.

"When I understood this, I made a decision: I would not be content watching others enjoy these things from afar. I would not accept a life of poverty. Instead, I would claim my share of the good things in life."

A Humble Beginning

"I was not born into wealth. My father was a simple merchant with a large family, and I had no inheritance waiting for me. I was not gifted with special intelligence or skills. So I knew that if I wanted to become rich, I would need time and knowledge."

"Time is something every man has equally. You all had the same time as I did to build wealth. Yet, you say you have nothing to show for it—except your families, which is something to be proud of."

Our teacher once said that knowledge has two parts: knowing facts and knowing how to discover what we don't know yet. So, I decided to learn how wealth is built, and once I understood it, I made it my mission to succeed."

A Life Worth Living

"Is it not wise to enjoy life while we can? Darkness awaits us in the afterlife, but today, we walk in the bright sun."

Key Takeaways

• **Hard Work Alone Does Not Guarantee Wealth.** Bansir and Kobbi realize that years of effort haven't made them rich. Simply working hard isn't enough—understanding how to grow and manage money is essential.

• **Wealth is About Income, Not Just Possessions.** Bansir envies Arkad's heavy purse, but Kobbi reminds him that true wealth comes from a steady flow of income, not just a pile of gold.

• **Ignorance About Money Keeps People Poor.** Both men admit they've never truly sought financial knowledge. They now see that wealth isn't about luck—it follows those who learn and apply sound financial principles.

• **Seeking Knowledge is the First Step to Wealth.** Bansir feels frustrated. This frustration helps him realize something important: to change his life, he must first change how he sees money.

- **Learn from Those Who Have Succeeded.** Instead of remaining in ignorance, Bansir and Kobbi decide to seek wisdom from Arkad. Having smart mentors around you is crucial for creating lasting wealth.

4

THE LESSON OF ALGAMISH

A Scribe's Struggles

"I found work as a scribe, carving records into clay tablets. I worked long hours, day after day, but despite my efforts, I had little to show for my earnings. Food, clothing, offerings to the gods, and other expenses consumed everything I made. But I did not lose hope."

"One day, Algamish, the money lender, came to the records hall. He needed a copy of the Ninth Law and demanded it be completed in two days. 'If you finish it on time,' he told me, 'I will pay you two copper coins.'"

"I worked as hard as I could, but the law was long, and when Algamish returned, the tablets were not finished. He was furious. If I had been his slave, he would have beaten me. But since the city master would not allow him to harm me, I stood my ground and made him an offer.

'Algamish, you are a very rich man. Teach me how to become rich, and I will work all night to finish your tablets. By morning, they will be ready.'"

"He looked at me, amused, and said, 'You are bold, but I accept your offer.'"

A Secret Worth More Than Gold

"All night, I worked, even as my back ached and my head pounded from the smoke of the oil lamp. When the sun rose, the tablets were complete."

"Now," I said, "tell me what you promised."

"You have kept your end of the bargain," Algamish replied. "And I will keep mine. I will tell you what I know because I am an old man, and old men like to talk. When young men seek the wisdom of their elders, they gain the knowledge of many years. But too often, young men believe that wisdom only applies to the past and fail to use it in their own lives.

The sun that shines today also shone when your father was born. It will shine again when your grandchildren grow old. Wisdom does not change.

'The thoughts of young men are like shooting stars—bright and fleeting. But the wisdom of age is like the stars in the night sky—steady and unchanging, guiding sailors on their journeys.

'Listen carefully, for if you do not grasp what I tell you, your night of hard work will have been wasted.'"

He looked at me with intense eyes and said in a serious

tone, "I found the path to wealth when I chose to keep a part of all I earned." And so will you.'"

The First Step to Wealth

"He paused, letting his words sink in. But I was confused. 'Is that all?' I asked."

"'That simple truth was enough to turn a poor shepherd into a wealthy money lender,' he replied."

"'But all the money I earn is mine to keep, isn't it?' I protested."

"'Far from it!' he said. 'You pay the cloth maker, the sandal maker, and the food seller. You give to the temple and to the wine merchant. But what do you keep for yourself? Look back at your earnings for the past year. What do you have to show for it? Nothing! You work for everyone but yourself. You might as well be a slave, working only for food and shelter.

'If you had saved just one-tenth of all you earned, how much wealth would you have after ten years?'"

Arkad's knowledge of numbers did not fail him, and he answered, "In ten years, I would have saved as much as I earn in one year."

"You are only half right," Algamish replied. "Every coin you save is a worker for you. The money it earns is its child, and that child can also work for you. If you want to become truly wealthy, your savings must earn, and their earnings must also earn. This is how wealth grows."

"You might feel cheated for your long night's work," he

said. "But if you truly understand what I've just shared, I've rewarded you a thousand times.""

"A part of everything you earn is yours to keep. It should be no less than one-tenth, but it can be more if you can afford it. Pay yourself first. Spend only what remains after you have saved. Buy clothes and food only after setting aside your savings. Give to the gods only after you have secured your own future."

The Seed of Wealth

"Wealth is like a tree. It starts from a tiny seed. The first coin you save is the seed from which your tree of wealth will grow. The sooner you plant the seed, the sooner the tree will grow. And if you continue to nourish it with regular savings, soon you will enjoy the shade of your wealth."

After saying this, Algamish took his tablets and left.

Arkad thought carefully about what the old man had told him. It made sense. So he decided to test it. Every time he was paid, he put aside one-tenth of his earnings and kept it hidden. Surprisingly, he didn't even notice the difference in his spending.

As his savings grew, he felt tempted to buy fine goods. Merchants brought treasures from distant lands, and he wanted them. But he resisted.

A Costly Mistake

A year later, Algamish returned and asked him, "Son, have you saved at least one-tenth of all you earned this past year?"

Proudly, Arkad answered, "Yes, master, I have."

"Good," Algamish said, "and what have you done with it?"

Arkad explained, "I gave it to Azmur, the brickmaker, who was traveling to Tyre. He promised to buy rare Phoenician jewels for me, which we would sell at a high price upon his return. Then we would split the profits."

Algamish sighed. "Every fool must learn," he said. "Why would you trust a brickmaker to know anything about jewels? Would you ask a breadmaker about the stars? No, you would go to an astrologer. If you wanted to learn about sheep, you would ask a shepherd. Yet, you trusted a brickmaker with your savings."

Learning from Mistakes

"Your money is gone. You have pulled your wealth tree out by the roots. But do not be discouraged—plant another. Save again. And next time, if you seek advice about jewels, ask a jeweler. If you seek knowledge about sheep, ask a shepherd. Advice is freely given, but be sure only to take what is valuable. If you follow advice from someone unskilled in wealth, you will pay for their mistakes with your own savings."

Saying this, Algamish left.

Arkad soon learned the painful truth of his words. The

Phoenicians had tricked Azmur, selling him worthless glass instead of real gems. His savings were lost.

But as Algamish had instructed, Arkad did not give up. He continued saving one-tenth of his earnings. Over time, it became a habit, and he no longer found it difficult.

The Road to Wealth

A year later, Algamish returned and asked, "What progress have you made since I last saw you?"

Arkad proudly answered, "I have continued saving, and this time, I entrusted my money to Agger, the shield maker. He buys bronze, and every four months, he pays me a share of his earnings."

"That is good," said Algamish. "And what do you do with the money he pays you?"

Arkad smiled, "I have grand feasts with honey, fine wine, and spiced cake. I have also bought myself a scarlet tunic. And someday, I will buy a young donkey to ride!"

Algamish laughed. "You are eating the children of your savings! How can your money grow if you spend all the earnings? First, build an army of golden workers. Then, when your wealth is great, you can feast without regret."

With those words, he left again.

A Final Visit from Algamish

Arkad did not see Algamish for another two years. When he

returned, he was much older, with deep lines on his face and heavy, tired eyes.

He asked, "Arkad, have you reached the wealth you once dreamed of?"

Arkad replied, "Not yet, but I have some wealth, and it continues to grow. And its earnings also grow."

"And do you still take advice from brickmakers?" Algamish asked with a knowing smile.

Arkad laughed. "When it comes to bricks, yes!"

"You have learned well," Algamish said. "First, you learned to live on less than you earn. Next, you learned to seek advice only from those skilled in wealth. And finally, you learned to make money work for you."

"You now understand how to acquire money, how to keep it, and how to use it. That makes you ready for a greater responsibility. I am old, and my sons care only for spending, not for earning. My businesses are vast, and I need someone I can trust to manage them."

"If you go to Nippur and take charge of my lands, I will make you my partner. You will share in my estate."

Arkad agreed. He had learned the three laws of wealth, which helped him boost Algamish's property value significantly.

When Algamish passed away, Arkad inherited part of his fortune as promised.

The Role of Luck vs. Preparation

When Arkad finished his story, one of his friends remarked, "You were lucky that Algamish made you his heir."

Arkad shook his head. "Luck had nothing to do with it. I had already proven my determination before I even met Algamish. For four years, I saved one-tenth of my earnings, even after losing my first year's savings. Is a fisherman lucky if he spends years learning fish habits? With every tide change, he knows just where to cast his net."

"Opportunity is a proud goddess who only visits those who are prepared."

The Power of Discipline

Another friend spoke up, "You had incredible willpower to keep saving even after losing your first year's earnings. That is rare."

Arkad shook his head again. "Willpower? No, my friend. Willpower is not about forcing yourself to lift an impossible weight. It is simply the discipline to follow through on the tasks you set for yourself. If I set a task, I complete it. That is why I choose my tasks wisely."

"If I told myself, 'For 100 days, I will pick up a pebble from the road and toss it into the river,' then I would do it. If I forgot one day, I would not say, 'I will throw in two pebbles tomorrow to make up for it.' No, I would go back and do it immediately. That is how I train myself to be reliable."

Is Wealth Limited?

Another friend asked, "If what you say is true, and it is so simple, then if everyone did it, would there be enough wealth for all?"

Arkad smiled. "Wealth grows wherever men put in effort. If a rich man builds a palace, does the gold he spends disappear? No! The brickmaker earns some, the laborers earn some, the artist earns some. And when the palace is finished, its value increases, as does the land around it. Wealth multiplies when it is wisely used."

The Time to Start is Now

Then another asked, "What should we do to become rich? We are no longer young, and we have nothing saved."

Arkad replied, "Start now. Follow the laws of wealth. It is never too late to grow your tree of gold."

"I advise you to take the wisdom of Algamish and say to yourself, 'A part of all I earn is mine to keep.' Say it in the morning when you wake up. Say it at noon. Say it at night. Say it every hour of every day. Repeat it until the words shine in your mind like letters of fire across the sky.

"Let this idea sink deep into your heart. Fill yourself with the thought. Then, choose an amount to save—let it be no less than one-tenth of your earnings—and set it aside. Adjust your other expenses if needed, but always keep that portion first. Soon, you will feel the pride of having a treasure that belongs to you alone. As it grows, so will your motivation. You will find new energy to work harder and earn more. And as your earnings increase, the amount you keep will also grow.

Making Money Work for You

"Then, make your treasure work for you. Money should not sit idle—it should be put to work, earning more money. Let your gold become your servant. Let its children and its children's children also work for you, multiplying your wealth over time.

"Plan for your future. Look at the elderly and remember that one day, you too will be among them. Invest your savings wisely so that you do not face old age with an empty purse. Be wary of offers that promise unusually high returns—they are often traps that lead to loss and regret.

"Also, ensure that your family is provided for in case the gods call you away. Making small, regular contributions is a smart way to secure their future. Waiting for a large sum of money might not be wise, as it may never arrive.

Seek Wisdom, Not Just Wealth

"Seek advice from wise men. Talk to those whose daily business is handling money. Let them guide you, so you do not make the same mistake I did when I trusted Azmur, the brickmaker, with my savings. A small but safe return is far better than a high-risk gamble that could leave you with nothing.

Enjoying Wealth Wisely

"Enjoy life while you are here. Do not be so obsessed with saving that you forget to live. If one-tenth of your earnings is all you can comfortably save, then be satisfied with that. Spend the rest wisely, and do not be so fearful of spending that you miss out on the joys of life. The world is full of wonderful things to experience—use your wealth to enjoy them, within reason."

The Moment of Realization

His friends thanked him and left. Some stayed quiet. They couldn't grasp the ideas because they lacked imagination. Some were bitter, believing that a man as rich as Arkad should simply share his fortune with his old friends.

But others left with a new light in their eyes. Now they saw why Algamish kept coming back to the scribe's room. He was watching a man move from ignorance to knowledge and from struggle to success. And when that man had finally found the light, a place in the world awaited him. No one could give him that place—it had to be earned.

A Lesson Passed Down

In the years that followed, these men often returned to Arkad. He welcomed them warmly, offering advice freely, as wise men are always happy to do. He helped them invest their savings wisely. This way, their money could earn steady returns. They avoided foolish or risky ventures.

For these men, their lives changed when they grasped a simple but powerful truth. This truth had traveled from Algamish to Arkad, and now from Arkad to them.

"A part of all you earn is yours to keep."

Key Takeaways

• **Pay Yourself First.** The foundation of wealth begins with saving at least one-tenth of your earnings. Before paying anyone else, secure your own financial future.

• **Make Your Money Work for You.** Saving alone is not enough. Wealth grows when your money is invested wisely, earning returns that continue to multiply over time.

• **Seek Knowledge from the Right People.** Bad advice leads to financial loss. Ask experts in their areas—jewelers for gems, shepherds for sheep, and savvy investors for money advice.

• **Discipline is the Key to Success.** Wealth grows with steady effort, smart choices, and good financial habits. Avoid the temptation to spend your savings on luxuries before they have multiplied.

• **Wealth is Created, Not Given.** Luck does not create lasting riches—preparedness and wise financial habits do. Those who seek knowledge and apply it will find wealth, just as Arkad did.

5

SEVEN CURES FOR A LEAN PURSE

The Wisdom Behind Babylon's Wealth

The glory of Babylon lives on. Over time, it has kept its reputation as the richest city, full of amazing treasures.

But it was not always this way. The riches of Babylon were the result of its people's wisdom. They had to learn how to build wealth.

When Good King Sargon came back to Babylon after beating the Elamites, he found a big problem. His Royal Chancellor explained it to him:

"For many years, our people thrived thanks to the impressive irrigation canals and temples you built, Your Majesty." But now that these projects are finished, people are struggling to support themselves."

"The laborers have no work. The merchants have few

customers. *The farmers cannot sell their crops. The people do not have enough gold to buy food."*

The King frowned. *"But where has all the gold gone that we spent on these great projects?"*

"I fear," the Chancellor replied, *"that it has ended up in the hands of a few very wealthy men. Most of our people let the gold slip through their fingers, just as goat's milk flows through a strainer. Now that the flow of gold has stopped, they have nothing to show for their earnings."*

The King was silent for a moment, deep in thought. Then he asked, *"Why have only a few men been able to keep all the gold?"*

"Because they know how," said the Chancellor. *"A man should not be blamed for his success simply because he understands the ways of wealth. And it would not be right to take away what he has earned fairly, just to give it to those who have less skill in handling money."*

"But why," the King demanded, *"shouldn't all people learn how to build wealth and become prosperous?"*

"It is possible, Your Majesty. But who can teach them? The priests know nothing of making money."

"Tell me, Chancellor," the King asked, *"who in all of Babylon knows best how to grow rich?"*

"Your question answers itself, Your Majesty. Who is the richest man in Babylon?"

"Well said!" the King agreed. *"It is Arkad. He is the wealthiest man in the city. Bring him before me tomorrow."*

The King's Plan

The next day, as the King had ordered, **Arkad** appeared before him. Though he was seventy years old, he still stood tall and full of energy.

"Arkad," the King said, *"is it true that you are the richest man in Babylon?"*

"So it is said, Your Majesty, and no one disputes it."

"How did you become so wealthy?"

"By taking advantage of opportunities that are available to all citizens of our great city."

"Did you have any wealth to start with?"

"No, Your Majesty. Only a strong desire for gold. That, and nothing more."

"Arkad," the King continued, *"our city is struggling. A few men know how to acquire wealth, but most of our citizens do not. Because they lack this knowledge, they cannot keep even a small portion of the gold they earn."*

"I want Babylon to be the wealthiest city in the world. To achieve this, we must become a city of many rich men. Therefore, we must teach all people how to build wealth."

"Tell me, Arkad, is there a secret to acquiring wealth? Can it be taught?"

"Yes, Your Majesty. The principles of wealth are practical and can be learned by anyone willing to listen and apply them."

The King's eyes brightened. *"Arkad, you have spoken the words I hoped to hear! Will you help us? "Will you teach these lessons to teachers? They will share this knowledge until every worthy citizen in my kingdom has learned it.""*

Arkad bowed. *"I am your humble servant, Your Majesty. Whatever knowledge I have, I will gladly share for the betterment of my fellow citizens and the glory of my King."*

"Then let my Chancellor gather one hundred men," the King commanded. *"Arkad will teach them how to build wealth. Let them learn well, so they may teach others."*

The First Lesson Begins

Two weeks later, the chosen one hundred men gathered in the Great Hall of the Temple of Learning. They sat on colorful rugs arranged in a semicircle. In the center, Arkad sat beside a small table, where a sacred lamp burned with a fragrant scent.

"Look, there he is," one student whispered to another. *"The richest man in Babylon. Yet, he looks just like any other man."*

Arkad rose to speak.

"As a loyal subject of our great King," he began, *"I stand before you to share the knowledge that made me wealthy."*

"Once, I was a poor young man who longed for gold. But I discovered certain principles that allowed me to acquire it. Now, by order of the King, I will share these principles with you."

"I did not have any special advantages when I started. The same opportunities that were available to me are available to every citizen of Babylon—including you."

"The first step to wealth begins with a fat purse. I once hated the sight of my own empty purse. I wanted it to be round and full, heavy with the weight of gold."

"So I searched for every possible remedy for a lean purse. I found seven."

"To you, who have gathered here, I will teach these seven cures for a lean purse—the same cures that made me wealthy."

"For the next seven days, I will explain one cure each day."

"Listen carefully. Debate these ideas with me. Discuss them among yourselves. Learn them well so that you may fill your own purses with gold."

"Once you have mastered these lessons, you will be ready to teach them to others."

"I will explain these principles in simple terms. This is the first step on the road to wealth, and no man can climb higher until he has mastered this first step."

"Now, let us begin with the first cure..."

The First Cure: Start Growing Your Wealth

Arkad turned to a thoughtful-looking man in the second row.

"My friend, what work do you do?"

"I am a scribe," the man replied. *"I carve records onto clay tablets."*

"Ah," Arkad said with a smile. *"I once did the same work to earn my first few copper coins. So, you have the same opportunity to build wealth as I did."*

He then looked at a broad-faced man sitting farther back.

"And what do you do to earn your living?"

"I am a butcher," the man answered. *"I buy goats from farm-*

ers, *slaughter them, sell the meat to housewives, and the hides to sandal makers."*

"Because you also work and earn," Arkad said, "you have every chance to succeed, just as I did."

In this way, Arkad asked each man about his trade, learning how they all earned their living. When he finished, he addressed them all:

"Now, my students, you see that there are many different ways to earn money. Each of your jobs provides you with a stream of income, flowing into your purse just like a river. Some streams are small, and some are large, depending on your skills and effort. Is this not true?"

The men nodded in agreement.

"Then," Arkad continued, "if each of you wants to build wealth, wouldn't it make sense to begin by using the income you already have?"

The students agreed.

Arkad then turned to a humble-looking man who had said he was an egg merchant.

"If you set aside one basket," Arkad asked, *"and put ten eggs in it each morning but take out only nine every evening, what do you think will happen?""*

"The basket will overflow with eggs," the man answered.
"Why?"

"Because each day, I put in one more egg than I take out."

Arkad turned to the class and smiled.

"How many of you have a purse that always feels empty?"

The students chuckled. Some lifted their purses in jest, showing their light weight.

"Now," Arkad said, "I will tell you the first remedy for an empty purse: Do exactly as the egg merchant. Every time you earn ten coins, spend only nine. Your purse will begin to grow heavier, and the weight of those extra coins will feel good in your hands. It will bring satisfaction to your soul."

"Do not laugh at the simplicity of this idea," he continued. "The truth is often simple. I promised to tell you how I built my fortune, and this was the first step. I, too, once had a lean purse and hated it. But when I began spending only nine-tenths of what I earned and keeping the rest, my purse started to fatten. And so will yours."

"Now, I will tell you something strange—though I do not fully understand why. When I stopped spending all my earnings, I found that I still got along just as well as before. I was not lacking anything. And, in time, gold came to me even more easily than before. It is almost as if the gods favor the man who keeps a portion of his earnings, while they avoid the man whose purse is always empty."

"Ask yourself: Do you like the short joy of buying fancy clothes, jewels, and food—things that don't last long?" Or do you prefer to build lasting wealth in the form of gold, land, investments, and a steady income?"

"The coins you spend will give you the first. The coins you keep will give you the second."

"This, my students, is the first cure for an empty purse: For every ten coins you earn, spend only nine. Debate this among yourselves, and if any man can prove it wrong, tell me tomorrow when we meet again."

The Second Cure: Control Your Spending

The next day, Arkad stood before his students once more.

"Some of you have asked me," he said, *"how can a man save one-tenth of his earnings when he's already spent all his money on necessary expenses?""*

He looked around the room.

"Tell me, how many of you had empty purses yesterday?"

"All of us," the students answered.

"Yet you do not all earn the same amount. Some of you earn much more than others. Some have large families to support, while others have few responsibilities. And yet, all of your purses were equally empty. Why is that?"

The students were silent.

"Now, I will tell you a truth about men and their money. No matter how much we earn, we always find a way to spend it all— unless we resist this habit."

"Do not confuse your 'necessary expenses' with your desires. Every one of you, along with your families, has more desires than your earnings can satisfy. So, your money is spent on these desires as much as possible. And yet, you still have many things you wish you could buy."

"All men desire more than they can afford. Even I, with my wealth, cannot satisfy every desire I have. There are limits to my time, my energy, and my needs. I cannot wear more than a few robes at a time. I cannot enjoy an endless feast. I cannot travel to every city in the world. And so, like you, I must choose which desires to satisfy and which to ignore."

"Just as weeds grow wherever there is space in a field, desires

will grow wherever there is the possibility of spending money. They will multiply endlessly if you let them."

"So, what must you do? You must study your spending habits. Look carefully at where your money goes. Many of your expenses may be unnecessary or wasteful. If you control them, you will find that you do not need as much money as you thought."

"Let this be your rule: For every coin you spend, demand full value in return."

"Write down everything you wish to buy. Then, separate your true needs from your desires. Limit your spending to nine-tenths of your earnings. Let the remaining one-tenth stay in your purse and grow."

"This one-tenth is your most important expense—it is the price you pay yourself for building wealth. Defend it fiercely. Adjust the rest of your budget as needed, but do not touch this sacred portion."

At this, a man in a fine red and gold robe stood up.

"I am a free man," he said. "I believe it is my right to enjoy life's pleasures. I refuse to be a slave to a budget that tells me how much I may spend and on what. I do not wish to live like a pack animal, carrying a burden!"

Arkad smiled.

"Who," he asked, "would create this budget for you?"

"I would, of course," the man replied.

"Ah," Arkad said. "If a pack donkey made his own budget, do you think he would include jewels, fine rugs, and heavy bars of gold? No. He would include only hay, grain, and water—things that truly sustain him."

"The purpose of a budget is not to restrict you but to help you.

It makes sure you have money for essentials, fun, and important wants—without wasting it on short-lived pleasures."

"Think of your budget as a guiding light in a dark cave. It helps you see the leaks in your purse and stop them before they drain away your wealth."

"Students, here's the second cure for an empty purse: Budget your expenses. This way, you can enjoy life, meet your needs, and grow your wealth. Just remember to spend less than nine-tenths of your earnings.""

The Third Cure: Make Your Money Work for You

"Look at your growing purse! You have learned to save at least one-tenth of everything you earn. You have also learned to control your spending to protect your growing wealth. Now, we must learn how to make your gold work for you."

"Gold sitting idle in your purse may bring comfort, but it earns nothing. The coins you save from your earnings are only the beginning. It is what they can earn that will truly build your fortune."

On the third day of his lessons, Arkad shared this wisdom with his students.

"So how do we put our gold to work?" he asked. *"My first attempt at investing was a failure—I lost everything. I will tell you that story later. But my first successful investment was a loan I made to Aggar, a shield maker."*

"Once a year, Aggar would buy large shipments of bronze from overseas to make his shields. Because he didn't have enough money to pay the merchants upfront, he borrowed from those who had

extra coins. He was an honest man who always repaid his debts, along with a fair interest, once he sold his shields."

"Every time I lent him money, I also reinvested the interest he paid me. Over time, not only did my original gold grow, but so did the money it earned. It was incredibly satisfying to see my wealth increase without additional effort from me."

"My students, a man's wealth is not just the coins he carries in his purse—it is the steady flow of income that constantly fills his purse. This is what every man desires: an income that continues to grow, whether he is working, traveling, or resting."

"I have become a very wealthy man because I built many sources of income. I learned about investing by lending money to Aggar. As I gained wealth, I made more investments. I also discovered new ways to grow my money."

"Think of gold as a worker. When you put your coins to work, they earn more gold. Over time, this new gold also starts working for you, creating an even greater income."

"To show you the power of this, let me tell you a story. A farmer, when his first son was born, took ten pieces of silver and gave them to a money lender. He asked the lender to invest it for his son until he reached the age of twenty. The money lender agreed to pay interest, adding one-fourth of the amount every four years."

By the time the boy was twenty, his ten pieces of silver grew to thirty and a half. This was due to compound interest. Since the young man didn't need the money yet, he left it with the lender to continue growing. By age fifty, his money grew to one hundred sixty-seven pieces of silver—seventeen times more than before!"

"This, my students, is the third cure for an empty purse: Put *your money to work. Let it earn more money for you, just as a flock of sheep grows by having more lambs. This steady income will ensure that your wealth constantly grows."*

The Fourth Cure: Protect Your Wealth from Loss

"Misfortune often strikes those who do not guard their gold carefully. If you do not protect your money, it will slip away from you just as easily as it came."

On the fourth day, Arkad warned his students about the risks of losing their hard-earned money.

"Once you begin to accumulate wealth, you will be tempted by many opportunities that promise great riches. Friends and family may urge you to invest in exciting ventures, but be cautious! The first rule of investing is to protect your money. Is it wise to chase high profits if you might lose your original investment? I say no! With great risk comes great chance of loss."

"Before you lend money to anyone, make sure they have the ability and reputation to repay you. Otherwise, you are not lending money—you are giving it away."

"Before you invest in any business, take time to understand the risks involved. Do not be blinded by dreams of quick wealth."

"Let me tell you a mistake I made in my early years. I saved money for a whole year. Then I gave it all to Azmur, a brick maker. He planned to travel across the sea to Tyre. There, he would buy rare Phoenician jewels for me to sell. He promised large profits. But the Phoenicians tricked him and sold him worthless pieces of glass instead. My entire fortune was lost."

"Looking back, I see my foolishness—I had trusted a brick

maker to buy jewels! What did a man who made bricks know about gems?"

"This painful lesson taught me to never trust my money with someone who is not skilled in the trade they are dealing in. Always seek advice from those who have experience in making money safely. Wise guidance is worth its weight in gold, especially if it saves you from bad investments."

"This, then, is the fourth cure for an empty purse: Guard your wealth from loss. Invest only where your money is safe, where you can reclaim it if needed, and where you are sure to earn a fair return. Seek the advice of wise and experienced men before making any investment."

The Fifth Cure: Invest in Your Own Home

"A man who saves nine-tenths of his earnings can enjoy life. If he invests some of that money wisely, his wealth will grow even faster.""

At their fifth lesson, Arkad spoke to his students about the importance of owning a home.

"Many men in Babylon rent homes. They pay a lot to land-lords. Yet, they live in cramped and dirty conditions." Their wives have no gardens to tend, and their children have no safe place to play except in the dirty streets."

"A man's family cannot fully enjoy life without a home of their own. There is great joy in eating fruit from your own trees and grapes from your own vines. A home provides security, pride, and motivation to work harder. That is why I say: Every man should own the house he lives in."

"Today, it is easier than ever to buy land. Our great king has expanded the city walls, creating more space for homes. The money lenders are willing to help those who wish to buy land and build houses. If you can save a reasonable portion of the cost, they will gladly lend you the rest."

"Then, instead of paying rent to a landlord, you will be paying off your own home. Each payment will reduce your debt, and in a few years, you will own your home outright. After that, your only expense will be the king's taxes."

"Your wife will care for the household more. She will also gladly go to the river to get water for the plants in your garden.""

"Owning a home brings many blessings. It lowers your living costs and frees up more of your earnings for other investments and pleasures."

"This, then, is the fifth cure for an empty purse: Own your own home."

The Sixth Cure: Secure Your Future Income

"Every man's life follows the same path—from childhood to old age. No one can escape this journey unless the gods call him early to the next world. That's why it's smart to plan for when you're not young anymore. You want to ensure your family is taken care of if you're not there to support them."

On the sixth day, Arkad spoke to his students about the importance of planning for the future.

"A man who understands the rules of wealth and builds his fortune must also think about the years ahead. He should make

wise investments that will last a long time and be available when he needs them most."

"There are different ways a man can secure his future. He may hide his gold in a secret place, but no matter how carefully he hides it, thieves may still find it. For this reason, I do not recommend this method."

"A man may also buy land or houses. If chosen wisely, these can hold their value and provide income or be sold when needed."

"Another way is to regularly deposit small amounts of money with a lender, allowing it to grow over time. Let me tell you about a sandal maker named Ansan. Eight years ago, he started saving just two pieces of silver each week. He deposited them with a money lender, who paid him interest. When he recently checked his account, his savings had grown to one thousand and forty pieces of silver!"

"If he keeps saving like this for another twelve years, his wealth will reach four thousand pieces of silver. That's enough to support him comfortably for life.""

"This example proves that even small, regular savings can create great wealth over time. Every man must plan for old age and protect his family, no matter his current success."

"I believe that one day, wise men will create a way for many people to contribute small amounts into a shared fund. This fund will provide a large payment to the family of anyone who passes away. Such a system would be a great blessing, as even a tiny contribution could create a secure future for one's loved ones. But since that day has not yet come, we must use the methods available to us now."

"So, my students, I urge you: plan ahead for your later years *and for the security of your family. Do not wait until it is too late, for a man who grows old without savings faces a harsh and bitter fate."*

"This, then, is the sixth cure for an empty purse: Plan for your future income so that you and your family will always have security."

The Seventh Cure: Increase Your Ability to Earn

"Today, my students, we discuss one of the most important cures for an empty purse. But we will not talk about gold—we will talk about you. For it is not only gold that determines a man's success, but his own abilities, habits, and decisions."

On the seventh day, Arkad addressed his class with a lesson that was more personal than financial.

"Not long ago, a young man came to me asking for a loan. When I asked why he needed money, he said his earnings were too low to cover his expenses. I told him that if he had no extra income, he would be a poor customer for a lender because he had no way to repay a debt."

"What you need, young man," I told him, *"is not a loan—you need to increase your earnings. What have you done to improve your skills and earn more?"*

"He answered that he had asked his employer for a raise six times in two months, but his request had been denied. He believed there was nothing more he could do."

"We may laugh at his approach, but he did have one important quality: a strong desire to earn more. And desire is the first

step to achievement. A man cannot succeed unless he truly wants to improve."

"But desire alone is not enough. It must be clear and specific. A man who only wishes to be rich is unlikely to succeed. But a man who sets a goal—perhaps to earn five gold pieces—can take steps to achieve it. Once he learns how to earn five, he can apply the same skills to earn ten, then twenty, and then a hundred. In this way, wealth is built, step by step."

"Desires must be simple and focused. If they are too many, too vague, or too far beyond a man's ability, they will only lead to frustration instead of success."

"The more skilled a man becomes, the more he can earn. When I was a humble scribe, I earned only a few coppers each day. I noticed that some scribes were paid more than I was, so I determined to be better than them. I studied their methods, worked harder, and improved my skills. Before long, I could carve more clay tablets in a day than any of them. My increased ability was quickly rewarded—I did not need to ask my employer six times for a raise!"

"Knowledge is the key to increasing wealth. A craftsman who learns from the best will become a master of his trade. A merchant who finds better goods at lower prices will make greater profits. A lawyer or doctor who studies and shares knowledge with others will become more skilled and respected in his field."

"The world is always changing, and those who stay still will be left behind. If you want success, you must constantly seek to improve yourself and your work. Strive to be among the best in your field, for men will always pay well for superior skill and knowledge."

"A man must also live with honor and wisdom. These things bring respect and lasting success:"

- *He must pay his debts on time and avoid buying what he cannot afford.*

- *He must take care of his family so they may love and respect him.*

- *He must prepare a will, so his wealth is properly passed on when he is gone.*

- *He must be kind to those in need and help where he can.*

- *He must show thoughtfulness to those he loves, for wealth alone does not bring happiness.*

"This, then, is the seventh cure for an empty purse: Improve yourself. Learn more, work harder, and act wisely so that you may achieve your goals and earn greater wealth."

Final Words from Arkad

"These, my students, are the seven cures for a lean purse. They are not just theories, but lessons from my own life—lessons that have made me the richest man in Babylon."

"There is more gold in this city than you can imagine, and there is enough for all who are willing to learn and apply these principles."

"Go forth and put these teachings into practice. If you follow them, you will prosper and grow wealthy, as is your right."

"And when you have succeeded, teach these truths to others, so that all honorable citizens may share in the wealth of our great city."

Key Takeaways

1 Save at Least One-Tenth of What You Earn – Pay yourself first. Set aside a portion of your income before spending on anything else. This is the foundation of wealth-building.

2 Control Your Spending. Avoid spending beyond your means. Identify necessary expenses and separate them from desires to ensure you are always saving.

3 Make Your Money Work for You. Simply saving money is not enough; invest it wisely so it can grow and create additional streams of income.

4 Protect Your Wealth from Los. Be cautious with investments. Only trust knowledgeable experts and avoid risky schemes that could wipe out your savings.

5 Invest in Your Own Home. Owning a home offers financial stability. It can lower living costs over time, and it provides security for your family. Instead of paying rent, work toward property ownership.

6 Plan for Your Future Income. Aging is unavoidable. So, get ready for the future. Invest for the long haul. Protect your finances and your family.

7 Increase Your Ability to Earn. Continuously improve your skills and knowledge. The more valuable you become, the greater your earning potential.

6

MEET THE GODDESS OF GOOD LUCK

"If a man is lucky, there's no telling how far his fortune may go. Throw him into the Euphrates, and he may swim out with a pearl in his hand." —Babylonian Proverb

The Search for Good Luck

The desire to be lucky is universal. It was just as strong in the hearts of men four thousand years ago in ancient Babylon as it is today. Everyone hopes to be favored by the mysterious Goddess of Good Luck.

But is there a way to not only catch her attention but also win her generous blessings? Is there a way to attract good fortune?

This was exactly what the men of ancient Babylon wanted to know. They were sharp thinkers and clever men.

That's why their city became the wealthiest and most powerful of its time.

Back then, there were no schools or universities. But they did have a place of learning, and it was a practical one. In the tall buildings of Babylon, one was as important as the king's palace, the Hanging Gardens, and the grand temples. You won't find much mention of it in history books—perhaps none at all—but it played a major role in shaping the wisdom of the time.

This was the Temple of Learning. Here, volunteer teachers shared knowledge from the past. Men gathered to discuss important topics openly. Inside its walls, all men were equals. Even the lowest slave could challenge the opinion of a royal prince without fear.

One of the most well-known visitors to the Temple of Learning was Arkad, the richest man in Babylon. He had a special meeting hall. Every evening, a crowd of men gathered there. Some were young, some old, but most were middle-aged. They debated interesting topics together.

Let us listen in and see if they knew how to attract good luck.

Does Luck Come from Gambling?

The sun had just set, glowing red through the dusty desert air, when Arkad arrived at his usual platform. Already, eighty men were seated on their small rugs, waiting for him. More were still arriving.

"What shall we discuss tonight?" Arkad asked.

After a short silence, a tall cloth weaver stood up. As was the custom, he spoke with respect. "I have a subject I would like to discuss, but I hesitate to bring it up for fear that it may seem foolish to you, Arkad, and to my good friends here."

Encouraged by Arkad and the others, he continued.

"Today, I was lucky—I found a purse filled with gold. Now, my greatest wish is to remain lucky. I feel that all men share this desire. So, I suggest we discuss how to attract good luck. Perhaps we can find ways to invite fortune into our lives."

"A very interesting subject," Arkad said. "One truly worth discussing.

"Some men believe good luck is just an accident, like stumbling upon a gold coin in the street. Others think it is a gift from the great goddess Ashtar, who rewards those who please her with her generous blessings.

"What do you think, my friends? Shall we seek to understand how to bring good luck into our lives?"

"Yes! Yes! And lots of it!" the crowd eagerly responded.

Arkad said, "Let's hear from those who found treasures— gold, jewels, or other valuable items—without any effort."

The room fell silent. Everyone looked around, expecting someone to speak. But no one did.

"No one?" Arkad said. "Then it seems this kind of good luck is quite rare. So, where else shall we look for it?"

The Illusion of Gambling

A young man in a fine robe stood up. "When we talk about luck, isn't it natural to think of the gambling tables? Isn't that where many men try to win the goddess's favor, hoping she will bless them with great riches?"

As he sat down, a voice called out, "Don't stop there! Tell us, did you find the goddess at the gambling tables? Did she make the dice fall in your favor so that you walked away with a heavy purse? Or did she let the dealer take your hard-earned silver?"

The young man laughed along with the others and replied, "I won't deny it—she didn't seem to notice I was there. But what about the rest of you? Have you found good fortune at the gambling tables? We are eager to hear and to learn."

"A good place to start," Arkad said. "We are here to consider all sides of this question. Ignoring gambling means missing out on something many men enjoy—the thrill of risking a little for the chance to win big."

"That reminds me of the chariot races yesterday!" another man called out. "If the goddess goes to the gambling tables, she must also visit the races. The chariots and galloping horses add even more excitement." Tell us, Arkad, did she whisper in your ear yesterday to bet on those grey horses from Nineveh? I stood behind you and could hardly believe my ears when I heard you place your bet on the greys! You know as well as the rest of us that no team in all of Assyria can outrun our beloved bay horses in a fair race.

"Did the goddess tell you to bet on the greys? She knew the black horse would stumble at the last turn. That's why our bays lost.""

The crowd burst into laughter. Arkad smiled and shook his head.

"Why should we believe the goddess of good fortune would take such an interest in one man's bet at a horse race?" he asked. "To me, she is a goddess of wisdom and generosity. She helps those in need and rewards those who deserve it.

"I do not expect to find her at the gambling tables or the races, where men lose far more gold than they win. I think she is found where men work hard and make smart choices. It's in those places that effort and good judgment lead to success.

The True Nature of Luck

"In farming, in honest trade, and in all kinds of work, there are always opportunities to make a profit. Not every effort will be successful, of course. Sometimes poor judgment leads to failure, and sometimes bad weather ruins a harvest. But in the long run, a hardworking man can expect to be rewarded. The odds are in his favor.

"But in gambling, the situation is reversed. The odds are never in the player's favor—they always favor the game master. The game is designed so that the keeper makes a generous profit from the money wagered by the players.

"Most players don't realize how certain the game master's

profit is—or how uncertain their own chances of winning really are.

"Consider a simple dice game," Arkad continued. "Every time you roll the dice, you bet on which side will land face-up. If the red side appears, the game master pays you four times your bet. But if any of the other five sides land face-up, you lose your money.

"So what do the numbers tell us? You have five chances to lose, but only four chances to win. This means that in the course of a night's play, the game master will keep, on average, one-fifth of all the money wagered.

"Can a man expect to win often when the odds are against him from the start?"

"Yet some men do win large sums at times," one listener pointed out.

"Yes, they do," Arkad admitted. "But here's my question— does money won through gambling bring lasting success?

"I know many wealthy men in Babylon, but I cannot name a single one who built his fortune by gambling.

"You who sit here tonight also know many successful men. I ask you—how many of them became rich from gambling? Let's hear their names."

A long silence followed. Then, someone joked, "Should we include the game masters?"

"If you can think of no one else," Arkad replied with a smile.

Where Does True Luck Come From?

"If none of you can name a single person who became wealthy from gambling, then what about yourselves?" Arkad asked. "Are there any among you who consistently win at games of chance, yet hesitate to recommend it as a way to build wealth?"

His question was met with groans from the back of the room, which quickly spread into laughter.

"It seems we are not looking for good luck in the right places," Arkad continued. "We have not found it in stumbling upon lost purses, nor have we found it at the gambling tables. As for the races, I must admit I have lost far more coins there than I have ever won.

"Now, let us turn our attention to our trades and businesses. When we successfully complete a profitable deal, do we call it luck? Or do we see it as a fair reward for our efforts?

"I believe we may be failing to recognize the gifts of the goddess. Perhaps she does help us, but we do not appreciate her generosity. Who would like to suggest another approach?"

The Cost of Hesitation

At that, an elderly merchant rose, smoothing his fine white robe.

"With your permission, honorable Arkad, and my fellow men, I have a suggestion," he said. If we attribute our business success to hard work and skill, what about the chances we almost took but missed?

"Think of the times when we were close to gaining something great, but because we hesitated, we missed out. If we had seized those moments, they would have been considered incredible luck. But since we failed to act, we cannot claim them as rewards for our efforts.

"Surely, many men here have such experiences to share."

"A wise suggestion," Arkad agreed. "Who among you has had good fortune within your grasp, only to see it slip away?"

Many hands were raised, including the merchant's. Arkad gestured for him to speak first.

"I'll share a story about how close good fortune can be to a man. Yet, he may let it slip away, leading to regret later," the merchant began.

A Missed Opportunity

"Many years ago, when I was a young man, newly married and just beginning to earn a good living, my father came to me with urgent advice.

"He told me about the son of a close friend who had discovered a barren piece of land just outside the city walls. The land was high above the canal, so no water could reach it.

"But this young man had a plan. He wanted to buy the land and build three large water wheels, powered by oxen, to lift water up from the canal. After irrigation, the land would be fertile. He planned to split it into small plots. Then, he would sell these plots to city dwellers wanting herb gardens.

"However, he did not have enough gold to complete the project. Like me, he was a young man with only a modest income. His father, like mine, had many children and little wealth.

He formed a group of twelve men. Each man agreed to invest one-tenth of his earnings into the project. They would do this until the land was ready to sell. The profits would then be shared fairly among them based on their contributions.

"'My son,' my father said to me, 'you are now a young man. It is my greatest wish to see you begin building a fortune so that you may one day be respected among men. I want you to learn from my mistakes and not repeat them.'

"'I deeply desire wealth, Father,' I replied.

"'Then let me give you this advice,' he continued. 'Do what I should have done at your age. Save one-tenth of your earnings and invest them wisely. If you do this, by the time you reach my age, you will have built a valuable estate.'

"'Your words are wise, Father, and I do desire riches. But my earnings are needed for many things. It is difficult to set aside even a little. I am still young. There is plenty of time.'

"'That is what I thought at your age,' my father warned. 'Yet many years have passed, and I still have not built my fortune.'

"'But times have changed, Father. I will avoid your mistakes.'

"'Opportunity is standing before you now, my son,' he

urged. 'It offers you a chance to build wealth. Do not delay. Go tomorrow to my friend's son and commit to investing one-tenth of your earnings. Do it without hesitation. Opportunity waits for no man. Today it is here—tomorrow it is gone. Do not miss your chance!'

"But despite my father's advice, I hesitated.

"That very day, merchants had arrived from the East with beautiful new robes—robes so rich and fine that my wife and I felt we *must* have them.

If I decided to invest one-tenth of my earnings, we would have to give up these luxuries and other things we really wanted.

"So I delayed my decision. And then, it was too late.

"The investment went forward without me, and it turned out to be far more profitable than anyone had imagined.

"This is my story—how I let good luck slip through my fingers."

Taking the First Step Toward Wealth

"In this story, we see how good luck comes to the man who seizes opportunity," commented a dark-skinned man from the desert.

"The path to wealth must always begin with a first step. That first step may be as simple as setting aside a few pieces of silver from one's earnings and making a small investment.

"I, myself, own many herds. But my fortune began when I was just a boy and used a single piece of silver to buy a young calf. That was the first step in building my wealth.

"Taking the first step—from earning money through work to having money work for you—is the key moment in a man's financial journey."

"Some men take that step early, and they outpace those who delay. Others, like the father of our merchant friend, never take it at all.

"If our friend the cloth weaver uses his new gold today, this luck will be just the start of even greater fortune.""

The Cost of Procrastination

At that moment, a stranger from another land stood up. "I am a Syrian," he said in broken Babylonian. "I do not speak your tongue so well. But I wish to give this merchant a name. Perhaps you will not think it polite. I do not know your word for it. If I say it in my language, you will not understand. So, tell me—what do you call a man who always delays doing what is good for him?"

"Procrastinator!" someone called out.

"Yes! That is him!" the Syrian exclaimed, waving his hands. "He does not seize opportunity when she comes! He waits! He says, 'I am busy now. I will think about it later.'

"But opportunity does not wait for slow men. If a man truly desires luck, he must act quickly. If he hesitates, he is a *procrastinator*, just like our merchant friend!"

The merchant stood and bowed good-naturedly as the crowd laughed. "I admire your honesty, stranger. Your words are true."

Another Tale of Opportunity

"And now," Arkad said, "let us hear another story. Who else has had opportunity knock, only to watch it slip away?"

"I have one," said a middle-aged man in a red robe. "I am a buyer of animals—mostly camels and horses, but sometimes sheep and goats.

"My story is about a time when opportunity came to me unexpectedly. Because I was unprepared, I let it slip away.

"Listen, and you shall judge for yourselves whether I was wise—or a fool."

"I had just returned to the city after a disappointing ten-day journey in search of camels. My mood was sour, and to make matters worse, I arrived at the gates just after they had been locked for the night.

"Frustrated, I resigned myself to camping outside until morning. While my slaves set up our tent, preparing for a night with little food and no water, an elderly farmer approached me. He, too, had been locked out of the city.

"'Honored sir,' he said, 'I see by your appearance that you are a buyer. If that is so, I would like to sell you my flock of sheep. They are excellent animals, freshly driven up from the pastures. But my wife is very ill with fever, and I must return home at once. Please, buy my sheep so that I and my slaves may mount our camels and travel back without delay.'"

An Opportunity Missed

"It was so dark that I could not see the farmer's flock, but from the sound of their bleating, I knew it was large.

"After wasting ten days searching for camels without success, I was eager to make a deal. The farmer, desperate to return home, offered me an excellent price. I accepted, knowing that my slaves could drive the flock into the city in the morning and sell it for a significant profit.

"Now that the deal was done, I called for torches to count the sheep. The farmer said there were nine hundred." I will not burden you with the difficulty we had in trying to count so many restless, thirsty animals in the dark—it was impossible. So, I told the farmer bluntly that I would count them at daylight and pay him then.

"'Please, honorable sir,' he pleaded, 'pay me just two-thirds of the price tonight so that I may be on my way. I will leave my most intelligent and trusted slave to assist with the count in the morning. He is honest, and you can give him the remaining payment then.'

"But I was stubborn and refused to make any payment that night.

"The next morning, before I awoke, the city gates opened, and four eager buyers rushed out in search of livestock. Because the city was on the verge of being besieged and food was becoming scarce, they were desperate to buy. They paid the old farmer nearly three times the price he had offered me.

"And just like that, my rare stroke of good luck slipped away."

The Lesson of Missed Opportunities

"A most unusual tale," Arkad commented. "What lesson can we learn from it?"

"The lesson," suggested an elderly saddle maker, "is that when we are convinced a deal is wise, we should act immediately.

"If an opportunity is good, then we must protect ourselves not only from others who may take it but also from our own hesitation. We humans are fickle creatures—we are far more likely to hesitate when we are right than when we are wrong.

"When we make a mistake, we stubbornly defend it. But when we recognize a good opportunity, we often hesitate, allowing it to slip away.

"That is why, when I see a good deal, I immediately put down a deposit. This protects me from my own weakness and saves me from later regretting the luck that should have been mine."

The Syrian's Bold Words

"Thank you! I wish to speak again!" The Syrian visitor was back on his feet.

"These stories are the same! Every time, opportunity

arrives with a good plan. And every time, these men hesitate! They do not say, 'Now is the best time! I must act quickly!'

"How can a man succeed with such thinking?"

"Wise words, my friend," agreed the livestock buyer. "Good luck slipped away from hesitation in both of these stories.

"But this is not unusual. The spirit of procrastination lives within all men.

"We all want wealth. But when an opportunity arises, a voice inside us whispers to wait, to delay, to think it over."

"And in doing so, we become our own worst enemies."

"I didn't know the word 'procrastination' when I was younger," the merchant said. "At first, I thought my missed opportunities were due to poor judgment. Later, I blamed my stubbornness.

"But eventually, I recognized the real enemy—a foolish habit of delaying action when quick action was needed.

"When I saw this hesitation for what it truly was, I hated it! I fought against it with all my strength, as a wild ass fights against the ropes that bind it to a chariot.

"And finally, I broke free."

Mastering Procrastination

"Thank you! I have a question for the merchant," said the Syrian.

"You wear fine robes. You do not look like a poor man. You speak like a successful man.

"Tell me, do you still listen when procrastination whispers in your ear?"

"Like our friend the buyer, I also had to recognize and conquer procrastination," the merchant replied.

"I realized it was my enemy—always waiting, always watching, always looking for a chance to block my progress.

"The story I shared tonight is only one of many examples of how it drove away my chances of success.

"But once I understood it, I defeated it.

"No man would willingly allow a thief to steal grain from his storage bins.

"No man would allow an enemy to drive away his customers and rob him of his profits.

"And when I realized that procrastination was doing the same to me—stealing my wealth and my future—I crushed it completely.

"Every man must conquer this enemy if he ever hopes to share in the riches of Babylon."

The Richest Man's Perspective

"What do you say, Arkad?" the merchant continued. "Many call you the luckiest man in Babylon because you are the richest.

"Do you think no man can find true success until he defeats procrastination?""

"It is exactly as you say," Arkad admitted.

"I have watched generations of men pass through the marketplaces, the trades, and the schools of knowledge.

"Opportunities come to all of them.

"Some take those chances and steadily work toward their biggest dreams."

"But the majority hesitate, falter, and fall behind."

Arkad turned to the cloth weaver.

"You suggested that we discuss good luck.

"Tell us—after this discussion, what do you now think of it?"

The cloth weaver stood up thoughtfully.

"I see good luck in a different way now," he admitted.

"Before, I thought of it as something that simply happened to a man without effort on his part.

"But now I understand that luck is not something one simply attracts.

"To bring good luck into one's life, a man must seize the opportunities that come his way.

"In the future, I will do my best to take advantage of such opportunities."

The True Nature of Good Luck

"You have understood the lesson well," Arkad replied.

"Good luck often follows opportunity, but it rarely comes without effort.

Our merchant friend would have had good luck if he had taken the chance the goddess offered him.

"Our livestock buyer, too, would have enjoyed good luck if he had closed the deal on the sheep and later sold them for a high profit.

"We set out tonight to discover how a man may attract good luck.

"And I believe we have found the answer.

"Both of these stories show how good luck follows opportunity.

"Nothing can change this truth: Good luck comes to those who seize opportunity.

"Those who are eager to take action for their own betterment attract the interest of the goddess of good fortune.

"She is always ready to help those who please her.

"And who pleases her most?

"Men of action.

"Action is what will lead you forward to the success you desire."

"Men of action are favored by the Goddess of Good Luck."

Key Takeaways

1 Luck Favors Action . Good fortune doesn't just happen by chance. It comes to those who act decisively when opportunities appear.

2 Gambling Is Not the Path to Wealth. Gambling and betting might look like quick ways to get rich, but they usually benefit the game master instead of the players. Wealth is built through effort and wise decisions, not by hoping for lucky wins.

3 Opportunities Are Easily Lost Through Hesitation.

Many people miss out on good luck. They often wait or hesitate when an opportunity comes up. Acting quickly and decisively is essential to success.

4 The Greatest Enemy of Wealth Is Procrastination. Those who delay action often miss their chance at financial success. Beating procrastination is key to creating wealth.

5 Good Luck Is Created, Not Given. Luck doesn't just happen. It's earned by those who seek knowledge, act, and make smart financial choices.

7

THE FIVE LAWS OF GOLD

Gold or Wisdom?

"A heavy bag of gold or a clay tablet inscribed with words of wisdom—if you had to choose, which would you take?"

By the flickering firelight, the sun-darkened faces of the listeners lit up with interest.

"The gold, the gold!" they all answered in unison.

Old Kalabab smiled knowingly.

"Listen," he said, raising his hand. "Do you hear the wild dogs howling in the night? They cry out in hunger, yet if you feed them, what do they do? They fight, they strut, then they fight again, giving no thought to the future.

"Men are the same. Given a choice between gold and wisdom, they ignore wisdom and waste the gold. And when it is gone, they wail in despair.

"But gold is only for those who understand its laws and follow them."

Kalabab pulled his white robe close around his legs as a cool night wind blew through the camp.

"You have served me well on our journey. You cared for my camels, worked hard in the desert, and fought off robbers. Tonight, I will share the tale of the five laws of gold." It is a tale unlike any you have ever heard before.

"Listen carefully to my words, for if you understand them and take them to heart, one day you shall have great wealth."

He paused, letting the weight of his words settle over them. Above them, the sky stretched deep and clear, stars shining bright in the desert night. Behind them, their tents stood tightly staked against the desert winds. Beside them, their neatly stacked goods were covered with animal skins. Nearby, camels rested. Some chewed contentedly while others snored.

The Story of Arkad's Son

"You have told us many good stories, Kalabab," said the chief packer. "We trust in your wisdom to guide us when our service with you is finished."

"Until now, I have only shared tales of my adventures in distant lands," Kalabab said. "But tonight, I will share the wisdom of Arkad, the wise and wealthy man."

"We have heard much of him," the chief packer said. "They say he was the richest man who ever lived in Babylon."

"He was indeed," Kalabab confirmed, "and that is because

he understood the ways of gold better than any man before or after him. Tonight, I will share the wisdom he passed down. His son, Nomasir, told me this many years ago in Nineveh when I was a young boy.

My master and I spent a long evening in Nomasir's palace. We brought him fine rugs, inspecting each one until he was happy with the colors. Finally pleased, he invited us to sit with him and drink a rare, fragrant wine—stronger than anything I had ever tasted.

"Then he shared with us the wisdom of his father, Arkad, just as I will now share it with you.

"In Babylon, it was customary for the sons of wealthy fathers to remain at home, waiting to inherit their family's fortune. But Arkad did not believe in this. When his son, Nomasir, came of age, Arkad summoned him and said:

'My son, I wish for you to inherit my wealth. But first, you must prove that you are capable of handling it wisely. Therefore, I ask you to go out into the world and show me that you can earn gold and gain the respect of other men.

To help you, I will give you two things that I myself was denied when I first set out as a poor young man trying to build a fortune.

First, I give you this bag of gold. If you use it wisely, it will be the foundation of your success.

Second, I give you this clay tablet, on which are written the five laws of gold. If you follow these laws, they will bring you wealth and security.

Ten years from today, return to me and tell me of your journey. If you have proven yourself worthy, I will name you as my heir. If not, I will give my wealth to the priests so they may bargain with the gods for my soul.'

"And so, Nomasir left to make his own way, carrying his bag of gold, the clay tablet carefully wrapped in silk, his slave, and his horses.

The Return of Nomasir

"Ten years passed, and as agreed, Nomasir returned to his father's house. In his honor, Arkad prepared a great feast and invited many friends and family members. After the feast, Arkad and his wife sat on their thrones in the great hall. Nomasir stood before them, ready to share his account.

"The evening air was thick with the smoke of oil lamps, casting a hazy glow over the room. Slaves in white tunics fanned the air with long palm leaves. The scene was one of majesty and dignity. Behind Nomasir, his wife and two young sons sat on fine rugs, eager to hear his tale.

"With great respect, Nomasir spoke.

'My father, I bow before your wisdom. Ten years ago, you sent me out into the world. I was on the brink of manhood, ready to forge my own path instead of living off your wealth.

You were generous, giving me both gold and wisdom. But I must confess—I did not handle the gold wisely. It vanished from my hands like a wild hare escaping from the grasp of an untrained hunter.'

"Arkad smiled patiently. 'Continue, my son. Your tale interests me.'

Lessons Learned Through Hardship

'I chose to go to Nineveh, a growing city where I believed I could find opportunities. Along the journey, I made many friends. Among them were two well-spoken men who owned a beautiful white horse, swift as the wind.

They told me of a wealthy man in Nineveh who owned a racehorse he believed was unbeatable. He was so confident that he would wager any sum that no other horse could outrun his. My new friends assured me that their horse was far superior and could easily win.

They invited me to join them in a bet. I was excited by the opportunity.

But our horse lost badly, and I lost a great deal of my gold.

"Arkad chuckled.

'Later, I learned the truth. The wealthy man was their partner. They traveled from city to city. They lured travelers into their trap and split the winnings. This trick taught me my first lesson in protecting my wealth.

I was soon to learn another, equally painful lesson. In our caravan was a young man from a wealthy family, much like myself. We became friends, and after we arrived in Nineveh, he told me of a merchant who had died, leaving behind a shop filled with fine goods. The shop could be purchased for a very low price.

He persuaded me to buy the business with my gold, promising that he would soon return to Babylon to collect his own money to help run it.

But he delayed his journey and proved to be a poor businessman. He spent foolishly and made bad deals. Eventually, I had to push him out, but by then, the business was ruined. I sold what was left for a pitiful sum.

After that, hard times followed. I had no trade or skill to earn a living. I was forced to sell my horses, my slave, and even my extra robes just to afford food and shelter. Each day, poverty crept closer.

But even in my darkest moments, I remembered your confidence in me, Father. You sent me out to become a man, and I was determined to do so.'

"Nomasir's mother buried her face and wept softly.

'Then I remembered the clay tablet you had given me, inscribed with the five laws of gold. I read your words carefully and realized that if I had followed them from the start, I would not have lost my fortune.

I memorized each law. I vowed that if luck smiled on me again, I would let experience guide me, not the foolishness of youth.

For the benefit of all who are gathered here tonight, I will now read the wisdom my father gave me, written on this tablet ten years ago.'

The Five Laws of Gold

1 Gold will come to anyone who saves at least one-tenth of their earnings. This habit helps build wealth for both the person and their family's future.

2 Gold works hard and grows for the wise owner who

finds profitable ways to invest it, multiplying like the flocks of the field.

3 Gold stays safe with the cautious owner who invests it under the guidance of those skilled in handling it.

4 Gold slips from anyone who invests in businesses or ventures they don't understand. It also escapes those who ignore advice from experienced people.

5 Gold avoids those who chase impossible profits, listen to schemers, or rely on their own inexperience and foolish hopes when investing.

The Five Laws of Gold in Action

"These," Nomasir declared, "are the five laws of gold as written by my father. I declare them to be worth far more than gold itself, as my story will prove."

He turned again to face his father. "I have told you of the hardships and despair that my lack of experience brought upon me," he said.

"But no misfortune lasts forever. My luck changed when I found work managing a crew of slaves building the new outer wall of the city.

"Remembering the first law of gold, I saved a small copper coin from my very first wages. I continued adding to it whenever I could, though progress was slow, as I still had to live. I spent my money carefully, determined to recover, before ten years had passed, the gold you had given me and that I had so foolishly lost.

Turning Savings into Wealth

"One day, the slave master, who had grown fond of me, said, 'You are a thrifty young man who does not waste what he earns. Have you saved gold that is not working for you?'

"'Yes,' I replied. 'More than anything, I wish to replace the gold my father gave me and that I lost.'

"'A worthy goal,' he said. 'But do you know that the gold you have saved can work for you and earn even more?'

"'I fear losing it again,' I admitted, 'as I lost my father's gold before.'

"'If you trust me,' he said, 'I will teach you how to handle gold wisely. In a year's time, this outer wall will be finished, and the great bronze gates must be built to protect the city from the king's enemies. There is not enough metal in all of Nineveh to make these gates, and the king has not prepared for it.

"'Here is my plan: A group of us will pool our gold and send a caravan to the distant copper and tin mines. We will bring the metal back to Nineveh. When the king commands that the gates be made, we alone will have the metal, and he will pay a high price. And if he does not, we will still own the metal, which can be sold for a fair profit.'

"I saw this as an opportunity to follow the third law of gold—investing under the guidance of wise men. And I was not disappointed. Our plan succeeded, and my small savings grew greatly from the profits.

The Power of Wise Investments

"In time, I became part of this same group in other ventures. These were men skilled in handling money wisely. They talked carefully about each business plan before they invested. They avoided reckless risks or unwise deals that could trap their gold in useless ventures. The silly choices I made—like betting on a horse race and teaming up with a novice partner—would not have gotten approval from these men. They would have pointed out their flaws immediately.

"Through my partnership with them, I learned how to safely invest money for steady profits. Over the years, my wealth grew faster and faster. I not only regained what I had lost, but I earned much more.

"Through my failures, struggles, and eventual success, I tested the five laws of gold time and time again, and I found them to be true.

"A man who does not understand these laws will rarely gain wealth, and if he does, it will quickly slip through his fingers. But the man who follows these laws will see gold come to him and work for him, like a faithful servant."

The Ultimate Lesson

As Nomasir finished speaking, he motioned to a slave standing in the back of the room. The slave stepped forward, carrying three heavy leather bags.

Nomasir took one bag and placed it before his father. "You gave me a bag of Babylonian gold," he said. "Now, I return to you a bag of Ninevite gold of equal weight. A fair exchange, as all can see."

Then, taking the other two bags, he placed them beside the first. "You also gave me a clay tablet filled with wisdom. In return, I give you two bags of gold."

He bowed respectfully. "This is to show you, Father, how much more valuable I consider your wisdom than gold itself. But can wisdom truly be measured in gold? Without wisdom, gold is quickly lost by those who have it. But with wisdom, gold can always be gained by those who do not have it, as these three bags before you prove.

"Father, it makes me truly happy to stand here today. Your wisdom has helped me become both wealthy and respected.""

Arkad placed a loving hand on his son's head. "You have learned well," he said. "I am indeed fortunate to have a son worthy of inheriting my wealth."

A Challenge to the Listeners

Kalabab paused and looked at his listeners.

"What does this tale of Nomasir mean to you?" he asked.

"Which of you can go to your father—or the father of your wife—and give an account of your earnings?

"What would these wise men think if you were to say: 'I have worked hard, traveled far, and learned much, yet I have little gold to show for it. Some I spent wisely, some I spent foolishly, and much I lost through poor choices'?

"Do you still believe it is simply luck that some men have wealth while others have none? If so, you are mistaken.

"Men who understand and follow the five laws of gold will always have wealth.

"Because I learned these five laws in my youth and followed them, I have become a rich merchant. I did not gain my wealth through luck or magic.

"Wealth that comes quickly also disappears quickly.

True wealth grows slowly, like a tree from a tiny seed. It brings real comfort and satisfaction over time.

"To earn wealth is not a burden to a thoughtful man. Carrying the burden year after year leads to great success.

"The five laws of gold offer great rewards to those who follow them.

"Each of these five laws carries deep meaning, and to ensure that their wisdom is not lost on you, I will now repeat them. I know them by heart, for when I was young, I recognized their value and would not rest until I had memorized them word for word."

The First Law of Gold

Gold comes easily to anyone who saves at least one-tenth of their earnings. This helps build wealth for themselves and their family.

A man who saves one-tenth of his earnings and invests it wisely will build a valuable estate. This estate will support him in the future and keep his family secure if he is no longer around. This law promises that gold will come gladly to such a man. I can confirm this from my own life. The more gold I save, the more easily it grows. The gold I set aside earns more, and that new gold earns even more in return. This is the power of the first law."

The Second Law of Gold

Gold rewards wise owners who invest it wisely, much like flocks thrive with good care.

"Gold is a willing servant. It is always eager to multiply when given the right opportunity. For every man who has saved a store of gold, opportunities will arise to make it grow. As the years pass, it increases in ways that often seem astonishing."

The Third Law of Gold

Gold stays with the careful owner who invests it wisely, under the guidance of those skilled in handling money.

"Gold remains with the cautious and flees from the reckless. A man seeking advice from gold experts learns to protect his wealth. He realizes it's better to keep it safe and let it grow slowly. Such a man enjoys the peace of mind that comes from knowing his wealth is secure and growing."

The Fourth Law of Gold

Gold vanishes from anyone who invests in businesses or

ventures they don't understand. It also disappears when they ignore advice from those skilled in managing money.

"A man with gold but little knowledge of how to use it will see many tempting opportunities that appear profitable. These investments often hide risks. If wise men looked closely, they would see a low chance of success. The inexperienced man trusts his judgment. He invests in businesses he doesn't understand. Often, he finds his judgment was wrong. Then, he pays for his mistake with his gold. The wise man, however, invests only after seeking advice from those who understand the ways of gold."

The Fifth Law of Gold

Gold avoids those who try to force it for unrealistic gains. It shuns tricksters and those who rely on their own naivety and false hopes.

"Every new owner of gold is approached with offers that sound like exciting adventures. These promises seem to give gold magical powers, making it grow at impossible speeds. But beware! Wise men know the risks that hide behind such dreams of quick riches.

Wealthy men of Nineveh were careful. They never risked their savings or invested in foolish ventures. They avoided deals that could trap their gold in worthlessness. Wealth grows slowly but surely with patience and smart investments, not through risky gambling."

What Will You Do with Your Gold?

"This concludes my tale of the five laws of gold," Kalabab said. "By sharing this with you, I have revealed the secrets of my own success.

"These are not secrets; they are truths every man must learn and follow to rise above daily struggles."

"Tomorrow, we will arrive in Babylon. Look! You can already see the eternal fire burning atop the Temple of Bel. We are nearing the golden city. Tomorrow, each of you will receive the gold you have so faithfully earned through your hard work.

"But I ask you—ten years from now, what will you be able to say about that gold?

"Will some among you, like Nomasir, use a portion of your gold to begin building wealth and follow the wisdom of Arkad? If so, I wager that ten years from now, you will be rich and respected among men, just as he was.

"Our wise choices follow us through life, bringing us joy and success. But just as surely, our foolish choices follow us, bringing regret and suffering. Nothing haunts a man more than the memories of opportunities he failed to seize.

"The treasures of Babylon are vast—so vast that no man can count their value in gold. And each year, they grow richer, waiting for men of purpose and determination to claim their share.

"There is great power in your desires. If you guide that power with the knowledge of the five laws of gold, you will earn your rightful share of Babylon's wealth."

Key Takeaways

1 **Wisdom is More Valuable Than Gold.** Without financial knowledge, wealth is easily lost. But with wisdom, gold can always be gained. Those who understand money will keep it; those who don't will waste it.

2 **Save Consistently.** Gold comes willingly to those who save at least one-tenth of their earnings. A strong financial base begins with smart saving.

3 **Make Money Work for You** – Gold grows when invested wisely. Rather than letting wealth sit idle, it should be put to work in profitable and secure ventures.

4 **Seek Knowledgeable Advice.** Gold belongs to those who invest wisely with the help of skilled experts. Ignorance leads to costly mistakes.

5 **Beware of Greedy and Foolish Investments.** Gold vanishes from those who seek quick profits, believe in get-rich-quick schemes, or invest in what they don't understand. True wealth is built patiently and steadily.

8

THE GOLD LENDER OF BABYLON

The Weight of Gold and Responsibility

Fifty pieces of gold! Never before had Rodan, a spearmaker of old Babylon, carried so much gold in his leather pouch. He walked cheerfully down the king's highway, fresh from the palace of His Majesty, the generous ruler. With every step, the gold clinked softly at his belt—the sweetest sound he had ever heard.

Fifty pieces of gold! All his! He could hardly believe his good fortune. What power these golden coins held! With them, he could buy anything—a grand house, land, cattle, camels, horses, even chariots. He could have anything he desired.

What should he do with it? As he turned onto a side street toward his sister's home, he wanted nothing more than to keep those heavy, shining coins for himself.

The Burden of Wealth

But a few days later, Rodan found himself troubled. He entered the shop of Mathon, the gold lender, who also dealt in jewels and rare fabrics. Rodan ignored the luxury items and headed straight to the back. There, Mathon relaxed on a fine rug, enjoying a meal served by a dark-skinned slave.

"I need your advice," Rodan said. He stood firm, feet apart, with his broad chest showing through his open leather vest.

Mathon, a thin man with a sallow face, smiled warmly. "What troubles have brought you to me, my friend? Have you lost money at the gambling tables? Or has some charming woman ensnared you? I have known you for many years, yet never have you come to me for help."

"No, no. It is nothing like that," Rodan said. "I do not need gold—I need your wisdom."

Mathon laughed. "Listen to this! No one comes to a gold lender for advice. My ears must be playing tricks on me!"

"They hear correctly," Rodan assured him.

"Can this be true? Rodan the spearmaker is wiser than all the others! He comes not for gold, but for guidance. Many men come to borrow gold to pay for their foolish mistakes, but they do not seek wisdom. And yet, who is better suited to give advice than a lender of gold, who hears the troubles of many men?"

Mathon clapped his hands. "You shall dine with me tonight," he said. "Andol," he called to the slave, "bring a rug for my honored guest, Rodan the spearmaker. Serve him a fine meal and fill my largest cup with the best wine. Let him eat and drink well!"

Once they were seated, Mathon asked, "Now, tell me, what troubles you?"

Gold Attracts Many Hands

"It is the king's gift," Rodan said.

"The king's gift?" Mathon repeated. "The king gave you a gift, and it troubles you? What kind of gift?"

"He was pleased with a new spearhead design I created for the royal guard. As a reward, he gave me fifty pieces of gold. And now I find myself deeply troubled."

"You are troubled by gold?" Mathon chuckled. "Surely, most men would envy your problem."

"But every hour of the day, someone comes to me asking for a share of it," Rodan explained.

"Ah, that is to be expected," Mathon said. "More men desire gold than possess it. And when they see someone gain it easily, they wish to take a part of it for themselves. But can you not simply say 'no'? Is your will not as strong as your arm?"

"I can refuse many of them," Rodan admitted. "But sometimes, it would be easier to say 'yes.' How can I refuse my own sister, to whom I am deeply devoted?"

"Surely, your own sister would not want to take away your well-earned reward," Mathon said.

"It is not for herself," Rodan explained. "She wants it for her husband, Araman. She dreams of him becoming a wealthy merchant. She believes he has never had a real chance to succeed, and she begs me to lend him this gold so he can start a business. She promises he will repay me from his future profits."

The Dangers of Lending to Friends and Family

Mathon nodded thoughtfully. "My friend, you bring a worthy question. Gold brings responsibility. It changes a man's place in the world. It brings fear—fear of losing it, fear of being tricked. It brings power—the power to do good. But it also brings dangers. Even the best intentions can lead a man into trouble."

He leaned forward. "Have you ever heard of the farmer of Nineveh who could understand the language of animals?"

Rodan frowned. "No, I have not. That is not the kind of tale men tell in the workshops of the bronze casters."

"Then I shall tell it to you," Mathon said. "Because when it comes to lending and borrowing, there is more at stake than just passing gold from one hand to another."

The Farmer Who Understood Animals

He began his story:

"Once, in Nineveh, there was a farmer who had a rare gift —he could understand what animals said to each other. Every evening, he would linger in the barnyard to listen to their conversations.

One night, he overheard the ox complaining to the donkey about his hard life.

'Every day, I pull the plow from morning until night,' the ox groaned. 'No matter how hot the sun burns, how tired my legs become, or how sore my neck is from the yoke, I must keep working. But you, my friend, live a life of leisure. You wear a beautiful blanket and carry our master wherever he pleases. And when he goes nowhere, you rest and eat fresh grass all day.'

The donkey, though known for his stubborn kicks, was a kind-hearted fellow.

'My friend,' he said, 'you do work hard, and I would like to help you. Here is what you must do: Tomorrow morning, when the servant comes to take you to the fields, lie on the ground and moan loudly. He will think you are sick and let you rest for the day.'

The ox followed this advice. The next morning, when the servant saw him lying there, he ran to tell the farmer, 'The ox is sick and cannot pull the plow.'

The farmer nodded. 'Then harness the donkey to the plow,' he said. 'The work must be done.'

And so, the donkey, who had only meant to help his friend, found himself doing the ox's job. All day long, he pulled the heavy plow. By evening, his legs were sore, his neck was chafed, and his heart was bitter.

That night, as the farmer listened once again, the ox said, 'You are a true friend! Thanks to your wise advice, I had a full day of rest.'

The donkey snorted. 'And I, like many others who try to help a friend, ended up carrying his burden. But I warn you —if you pretend to be sick again, I overheard the master telling the servant to send for the butcher. And I would be glad if he did, for you are a lazy beast!'

From that day on, the ox never pretended to be sick again. And the two were no longer friends."

The Lesson of the Story

Mathon looked at Rodan. "Can you tell me the lesson of this story?"

Rodan thought for a moment. "It is a good tale," he admitted. "But I do not see the lesson."

Mathon smiled. "It is simple. If you wish to help a friend, do so in a way that does not place his burden on your own shoulders."

Rodan nodded slowly. "I had not thought of it that way. I do not wish to take on my sister's husband's struggles. But tell me, you lend to many people. Do they always repay?"

Mathon chuckled, his eyes gleaming with experience. "Would I be a wise lender if I gave gold to those who could not repay? A lender must think hard about how his gold will be used. Will it be spent wisely and returned? Or will it be wasted, hurting both the lender and the borrower?"

He pulled a long, red leather chest from beneath a table. "Let me show you my token chest. It will tell you many stories."

The Gold Lender's Token Chest

"My token chest teaches me that the safest loans are given to those who already own valuable possessions. These people have land, jewels, camels, or other assets they could sell to repay their debt. Some of the tokens I keep are valuable jewels, worth more than the loan itself. Others are promises that if the loan is not repaid as agreed, the borrower will give me a portion of their property. With such loans, I am confident my gold will be returned, along with the interest I am owed, because the loan is secured by property.

"Another group consists of those who have the ability to earn. They are workers like you, Rodan—those who labor or provide services and receive payment for their efforts. As long as they are honest and do not suffer misfortune, I know they can repay what they borrow, along with my rightful interest. These loans are based on human effort.

"Then there are those who have neither property nor a steady income. Life is difficult, and there will always be some who cannot manage it well. When I lend them money, even a small amount, my token chest warns me. It reminds me that I might never get my gold back. This is only if their debt isn't backed by a reliable friend who knows they are honest."

Mathon unfastened the clasp and opened the lid of the chest. Rodan leaned forward eagerly.

Stories from the Token Chest

At the top of the chest, resting on a scarlet cloth, was a bronze necklace. Mathon picked it up and stroked it gently. "This shall always remain in my token chest because its owner has passed into the great darkness. I treasure this token, just as I treasure his memory, for he was my dear friend. We were successful trading partners for many years. But then he brought a woman from the east to be his wife—beautiful, but unlike the women of our land. She was dazzling, and he spent his gold lavishly to satisfy her desires.

"When his gold was gone, he came to me in distress. I advised him to take control of his finances again. He swore by the Great Bull that he would. But fate had other plans. In a quarrel, she plunged a knife into his heart after he dared her to do it."

"And what became of her?" Rodan asked.

Mathon held up the scarlet cloth. "This was hers," he said. "Overcome with guilt, she threw herself into the Euphrates. These two loans will never be repaid. My token chest teaches me that people overwhelmed by strong emotions are not safe risks for a lender of gold."

He set the cloth aside and picked up a ring carved from ox bone. "This, however, is a different story," he said. "It belongs to a farmer. His family weaves rugs, which I buy from them. One year, locusts came, and they had no food. I lent him gold, and when his crops were harvested, he repaid me.

"Later, he returned with an idea. A traveler had told him of goats from a distant land with long, fine hair that could be woven into rugs more beautiful than any in Babylon. He wanted to buy a herd, but he had no money. So, I lent him gold for the journey. Now, his herd is growing, and next year, I will surprise the nobles of Babylon with the finest rugs they have ever seen. Soon, I will return this ring to him, for he insists on repaying promptly."

"Do some borrowers actually repay so faithfully?" Rodan asked.

"If they borrow for a purpose that brings money back to them, then yes," Mathon replied. "But if they borrow because of their foolishness, you must be cautious if you ever wish to see your gold again."

The Cost of Reckless Borrowing

Rodan picked up a heavy gold bracelet encrusted with rare jewels. "Tell me about this," he said.

Mathon chuckled. "I see the women of Babylon appeal to you, my friend."

Rodan laughed. "I am much younger than you, Mathon."

"That may be true, but this time, you suspect romance where there is none. The owner of this bracelet is an old, wrinkled woman who talks endlessly yet says nothing of importance. Once, her family was wealthy and good customers of mine, but hard times fell upon them. She has a son, whom she dreams of making into a great merchant.

"She borrowed gold to help him enter a partnership with a caravan trader. This trader, however, turned out to be a scoundrel. He abandoned the poor boy in a distant city, taking all the money and leaving him with nothing.

"Perhaps one day, when the boy grows into a man, he will repay the debt. Until then, I receive no interest on this loan—only endless chatter from his mother. But at least the jewels in this bracelet are worth the loan."

"Did she ask for your advice before taking the loan?" Rodan inquired.

Mathon shook his head. "Not at all. She had already imagined her son as a powerful merchant. To suggest otherwise offended her greatly. I knew the risks, but she offered good security, so I could not refuse her."

The Lender's Dilemma

He picked up a simple piece of knotted rope. "This belongs to Nebatur, the camel trader. When he wishes to buy a herd larger than his funds allow, he brings me this knot, and I lend him gold. He is a wise trader, and I trust his judgment. Many merchants of Babylon have my confidence because they are honorable. Their tokens come and go from my chest frequently. Good merchants are an asset to the city, and it profits me to help them keep trade flowing so that Babylon remains prosperous."

Mathon then picked up a small beetle carved from turquoise and tossed it aside with disgust. "A worthless trinket from Egypt," he said. "The boy who owns this does not care if he ever repays me. When I ask him for my gold, he shrugs and says, 'How can I repay when bad luck follows me? You have plenty more gold.'

"What can I do? The token belongs to his father—a hardworking man of modest means who pledged his land and cattle to secure his son's ventures. At first, the young man found success, but in his eagerness to grow rich quickly, he made reckless decisions. His businesses collapsed.

"Youth is ambitious. Youth seeks shortcuts to wealth. But without experience, it does not see that debt is a deep pit— one can fall in quickly, but climbing out takes great effort. Debt brings sorrow, regret, and restless nights.

"Yet, I do not discourage borrowing gold. In fact, I encourage it—when it serves a wise purpose. My own success as a merchant began with borrowed gold.

"But what should a lender do in a case like this? The young man has lost all hope. He does nothing to recover. He is discouraged and makes no effort to repay. My heart hesitates to take his father's land and cattle from him."

The Risk of Lending to the Unprepared

Rodan listened closely. "Your stories are fascinating, Mathon," he said, "but you still have not answered my question. Should I lend my fifty pieces of gold to my sister's husband? That money means a great deal to me."

Mathon nodded. "Your sister is a good woman, whom I

respect greatly. But if her husband came to me seeking a loan, I would ask him: 'For what purpose do you need this gold?'

"If he answered that he wanted to become a merchant like me—dealing in jewels and fine goods—I would ask, 'Do you know how to trade? Do you know where to buy at the lowest price and where to sell for a profit?' Could he answer 'yes' to these questions?"

"No, he could not," Rodan admitted. "He has helped me with making spears, and he has done some work in the markets, but he has no real experience."

"Then I would tell him his plan is unwise," Mathon said. "A merchant must learn his trade. His ambition is good, but his knowledge is lacking. I would not lend him gold.

"You see, Rodan, gold is the merchant's stock. It is easy to lend, but if lent unwisely, it is difficult to recover. A wise lender does not take risks—he ensures repayment.

"It is good to help those in need, but help must be given wisely. Otherwise, like the farmer's donkey, we may take on burdens that do not belong to us."

The True Value of Fifty Pieces of Gold

"I have wandered from your question again, Rodan," Mathon admitted. "But here is my answer: Keep your fifty pieces of gold. What you have earned through your hard work and what has been given to you as a reward is yours alone. No one has the right to demand it from you unless it is truly your choice to give it. If you wish to lend it so that it may earn more gold, then do so carefully, spreading your risk across multiple places. I do not like gold sitting idle, but I dislike reckless risk even more.

"How many years have you worked as a spearmaker?"

"Three years."

"And how much have you saved, besides the king's gift?"

"Three gold pieces."

"So each year you have worked hard, denying yourself many comforts, just to save one piece of gold?"

"That is true."

"Think about this: If you keep saving like this, in fifty years, you'll have saved fifty pieces of gold. That's a lifetime of work!""

Rodan's eyes widened. "A lifetime of work," he repeated.

"Do you think your sister would risk her savings? It took you fifty years of hard work to earn that money. All for her husband to try becoming a merchant?""

"Not if I explained it to her the way you just did."

"Then go to her and say: 'For three years, I have worked every day except fast days, from morning until night. I have denied myself many things that my heart desired, just so that for each year of work, I could save one single piece of gold. You are my beloved sister, and I truly want your husband to succeed in business. If he presents me with a plan that seems wise and realistic to my friend Mathon, I will gladly lend him my savings of an entire year. That way, he has an opportunity to prove that he can succeed.'

"If he has the ability to succeed, he will prove it. If he fails, he will not owe you more than he could reasonably hope to repay one day.

The Final Advice

"I am a gold lender because I own more gold than I need for my own trade. I want my extra gold to work for others and earn me more gold in return. But I will not lend it where I am not confident it is safe and will be repaid. Nor will I lend it where I am unsure I will receive the interest I am owed.

"I have shared with you, Rodan, some of the lessons from my token chest. Through them, you can see the weakness of men—their eagerness to borrow gold, even when they have no real means to repay it. Now you see that their dreams of riches are often just empty hopes. They lack the skills needed to make those dreams real.

"You, Rodan, now hold gold in your hands, and you must make it work for you. You are about to become, in a way, a lender of gold. If you protect your treasure wisely, it will grow and bring you great pleasure and profit throughout your life. But if you let it slip away, you will spend your days in regret.

"Tell me, Rodan, what do you desire most for this gold in your pouch?"

"To keep it safe," Rodan answered without hesitation.

"A wise answer," Mathon said approvingly. "Your first concern is safety. Do you truly believe your sister's husband would keep it safe?"

Rodan hesitated. "I fear not, for he does not have the wisdom to protect gold."

"Then do not let yourself be swayed by feelings of obligation. Do not entrust your gold to anyone who may lose it. If you wish to help your family or friends, find another way—one that does not put your treasure at risk. Never forget that gold disappears quickly in the hands of those who do not know how to guard it. It would be just as wasteful to throw your gold away on extravagance as it would be to let others lose it for you.

"After safety, what do you want most from your gold?"

"For it to earn more gold."

"Again, you speak wisely. Gold should be put to work so that it multiplies. A wisely invested sum can double before a man reaches old age. But if you risk losing it, you also risk losing all the wealth it could have earned for you.

"Do not be tempted by wild promises of enormous profits from men with impractical schemes. Such plans are the dreams of those who do not understand the safe and steady rules of trade. Be realistic in what you expect your gold to earn, so that you may keep it and enjoy its benefits. To lend it with a promise of outrageously high returns is to invite loss.

"Instead, look for partners who are already successful men and businesses." Let your gold be used by those who are skilled and experienced, so that it earns well while being safely managed.

"This is how you avoid the misfortunes that ruin so many men to whom the gods have entrusted gold."

Rodan opened his mouth to thank Mathon for his wise advice, but the old lender waved his words away.

"The king's gift will teach you much wisdom, Rodan. If

you wish to keep your fifty pieces of gold, you must be extremely careful. Many temptations will arise. Many people will offer advice. Many opportunities will promise great profits. Let my stories from the token chest warn you: before you part with any gold, make sure you can safely get it back.

"If you ever wish for more advice, return to me. I will gladly give it."

As Rodan turned to leave, Mathon gestured to the inside lid of his token chest. "Before you go, read what I have carved here. It applies to both the borrower and the lender alike."

Rodan leaned in and read the inscription:

BETTER A LITTLE CAUTION THAN A GREAT REGRET.

Key Takeaways

1 **Wealth Brings Responsibility.** Gold is a powerful tool, but it must be managed wisely. The more wealth one has, the more people will seek to share in it.

2 **Lend with Caution.** Helping friends or family with money can be risky. If they lack experience or a solid plan, lending them gold may only lead to loss and regret.

3 **Gold Must Be Protected.** A wise man does not entrust his gold to those who do not know how to safeguard or grow it. Money should only be lent to those who can repay it.

4 **Invest with Knowledge, Not Emotion.** Many people borrow money based on dreams rather than experience. A

lender must carefully judge if a borrower has the ability and discipline to succeed.

5 Gold Should Multiply, Not Be Wasted. Gold should not sit idle, nor should it be risked in foolish ventures. A wise person makes it work through steady, secure investments.

9

THE WALLS OF BABYLON

The Siege of Babylon

Old Banzar, a hardened warrior from another time, stood guard at the passage leading to the top of Babylon's ancient walls. Above him, brave defenders fought fiercely to protect the city. The future of Babylon—home to hundreds of thousands—depended on them.

Beyond the walls, the enemy's war cries filled the air. The ground trembled under the hooves of countless horses. The deafening crash of battering rams echoed as they pounded the city's great bronze gates.

Inside the streets, behind the gates, spearmen waited, ready to defend the entrance if the gates failed. But their numbers were small. The main army of Babylon, along with the king, was far away in the east, waging war against the Elamites. No one had expected an attack while they were gone. Now, the mighty Assyrian army had arrived from the north, and Babylon's survival rested on its walls.

The Fear of the People

Terrified citizens crowded around Banzar. Their faces were pale with fear. They were desperate for news about the battle. They watched in horror as wounded and dead soldiers were carried down from the walls.

This was the enemy's main attack point. After circling the city for three days, they had finally thrown their full force against this section and this gate.

From the top of the wall, defenders fought hard. They pushed back the enemy's climbing platforms. They knocked down ladders with arrows and burned oil. If needed, they used spears too. Meanwhile, thousands of enemy archers unleashed a deadly rain of arrows upon them.

Banzar had the best view of the battle. He was closest to the action and the first to hear of each successful defense.

Reassuring the City

An elderly merchant pushed through the crowd, his trembling hands clutching at Banzar. "Tell me! Tell me!" he begged. "They won't get in, will they? My sons are with the king—there's no one left to protect my wife. If the enemy breaks through, they'll steal everything I own. They'll take all our food, and we're too old to defend ourselves—too old even to be slaves. We will starve. We will die. Tell me they cannot get in!"

"Calm yourself, good merchant," Banzar reassured him. "The walls of Babylon are strong. Go back to the marketplace and tell your wife that these walls will protect you, just as they protect the king's treasures. Stay close to the walls so that stray arrows do not strike you!"

As the merchant stepped back, a woman holding a baby took his place. "Sergeant, what news from the top?" she asked. "Tell me the truth, so I can ease my poor husband's mind. He lies in bed with a bad fever from his wounds. Still, he wants to wear his armor and keep his spear close. He does this to protect me and our unborn child. He says the enemy will be merciless if they get inside."

"Take heart, mother," Banzar told her. "The walls of Babylon will protect you and your children. They are high and strong. Can you not hear our brave soldiers as they pour boiling oil onto the enemy's ladders?"

"Yes, I hear them," she said. "But I also hear the battering rams slamming against our gates."

"Go back to your husband and tell him the gates are strong. They will hold against the rams. And the enemy that climbs our walls only reaches the sharp end of a defender's spear. Now hurry—stay close to the buildings and out of sight!"

The Innocence of a Child

As reinforcements arrived, Banzar stepped aside to let them pass. Their bronze shields clanked together as they marched in heavy formation toward the walls.

A small girl tugged at Banzar's belt. "Please, soldier, tell me—are we safe?" she asked in a trembling voice. "The noises are so terrible. I see the men bleeding. I'm so scared. What will happen to my family—my mother, my little brother, and the baby?"

The battle-hardened soldier blinked, his heart softening at the sight of the child.

"Do not be afraid, little one," he said gently. "The walls of Babylon will protect you, your mother, and your baby brother. Over a hundred years ago, Queen Semiramis built these walls to keep us safe. Never once have they been broken through. Go back and tell your mother and brother that they have nothing to fear."

The Triumph of Babylon

Banzar stood at his post every day. He watched wave after wave of reinforcements march up to fight. Many returned wounded or lifeless. Terrified citizens gathered around him, all desperate for hope.

To each, he gave the same unwavering answer: "The walls of Babylon will protect you."

For three weeks and five days, the battle raged without rest. Blood soaked the ground behind Banzar, turning the dirt into mud as the wounded were carried away. Each day, enemy corpses piled up by the walls. Each night, comrades dragged them away to bury them.

Finally, on the fifth night of the fourth week, the noise outside began to fade. As the first rays of daylight stretched across the plains, great clouds of dust rose in the distance. The enemy was retreating.

A triumphant cheer erupted from the defenders. There was no mistaking its meaning. The victorious cry spread to the troops behind the walls, then to the streets of Babylon. It rolled across the city like a mighty storm.

People poured from their homes, flooding the streets in celebration. The fear that had gripped them for weeks was released in a wild chorus of joy.

From the top of the Temple of Bel, a great fire was lit, its flames stretching toward the sky. A column of blue smoke drifted high above the city, carrying the message of victory far and wide.

Once again, the mighty walls of Babylon had stood strong, repelling a powerful and ruthless enemy. The invaders had come to plunder Babylon's wealth and enslave its people—but the city endured, just as it had for centuries.

Babylon thrived because it was well protected. It could not afford to be otherwise.

The walls of Babylon were a powerful symbol of humanity's need for security. That need has not changed—it is just as strong today as it was then. But today, we have different ways to protect ourselves.

Now, instead of stone walls, we build financial security

through insurance, savings, and wise investments. These serve as our modern-day defenses, shielding us from life's unexpected hardships.

WE CANNOT AFFORD TO BE WITHOUT ADEQUATE PROTECTION.

Key Takeaways

1 **Strong Defenses Ensure Survival.** The walls of Babylon symbolize the importance of protection. Modern people must protect their well-being, just as defenders once did. They need financial security, savings, and readiness for what comes next.

2 **Fear is Natural, but Preparation Brings Confidence.** The citizens of Babylon were terrified, but their trust in the city's defenses reassured them. Preparation in life helps reduce anxiety during tough times. This can be through financial planning or managing risks.

3 **Endurance Leads to Victory.** The siege lasted for weeks, but Babylon withstood the assault. Similarly, resilience in the face of financial or personal hardships ensures long-term stability and success.

4 **Security Must Be a Priority.** Babylon thrived because it invested in its defenses. In today's world, a solid financial foundation is key. Smart investments, insurance, and savings shield you from surprises.

5 The Principles of Protection Are Timeless. Once, physical walls offered safety. Now, financial stability provides security. The lesson remains the same: **we cannot afford to be without adequate protection.**

10

THE CAMEL TRADER OF BABYLON

A Hungry Mind Sees Clearly

The hungrier a person gets, the clearer their mind works—though they also become more sensitive to the smell of food.

Tarkad, the son of Azure, knew this all too well. He hadn't eaten anything for two whole days except for two small figs he had stolen from a garden. He had tried to grab more, but an angry woman had rushed out, yelling and chasing him down the street. Her loud, angry voice still rang in his ears as he walked through the marketplace. It reminded him to keep his hands to himself, no matter how tempting the fruits in the baskets looked.

He had never noticed before just how much food was sold in the markets of Babylon, nor how good it all smelled. Leaving the market behind, he wandered over to an inn and paced back and forth outside. Maybe he would run into someone he knew—someone who might lend him a copper coin. If he had a copper, he knew the innkeeper might smile at him and serve him a generous meal. Without it, he was certain he would be unwelcome.

An Unwelcome Encounter

Lost in thought, he suddenly found himself face to face with the last person he wanted to see: Dabasir, the camel trader. Of all the people Tarkad borrowed from, Dabasir made him feel the worst. This was mainly because Tarkad never paid him back as promised.

Dabasir's face lit up when he saw him. "Ah! Tarkad! Just the man I was looking for! You still owe me two pieces of copper from a month ago, and before that, a piece of silver. What luck to find you today! I could really use those coins right now. What do you say, boy?"

Tarkad stammered, his face turning red. He was too weak from hunger to argue with Dabasir's bluntness. "I'm sorry, really sorry," he mumbled. "But I have neither copper nor silver to pay you today."

"Then get it," Dabasir said firmly. "Surely you can find a few coins to repay a friend of your father who helped you when you were in need?"

"It's not my fault," Tarkad said weakly. "Bad luck follows me, and that's why I can't pay."

"Bad luck?" Dabasir scoffed. "You'd blame the gods for your own choices? Bad luck follows every man who borrows more than he repays. Come with me while I eat—I'm hungry, and I have a story to tell you."

Tarkad winced at Dabasir's harsh words, but at least he was being invited into the inn.

A Lesson Over a Meal

Inside, Dabasir led him to a far corner where they sat on small rugs. When the innkeeper, Kauskor, approached, Dabasir called out loudly, "Fat lizard of the desert! Bring me a leg of goat, cooked well with lots of juice, along with bread and vegetables—I'm hungry and need a big meal. And bring my friend here a jug of water. Make sure it's cool, for the day is hot."

Tarkad's heart sank. Would he really have to sit here, drinking only water, while watching Dabasir eat an entire goat leg? He said nothing—what could he say?

Dabasir, on the other hand, was in high spirits. Smiling and waving to the other diners, he continued chatting. "I heard from a traveler just back from Urfa about a rich man who has a piece of stone so thin you can see through it. He placed it in his window to keep out the rain. It's yellow, and when he looked through it, the whole world outside looked strange, not as it really is. What do you think of that, Tarkad? Do you believe a man could see the world in a different color than it truly is?"

"I suppose so," Tarkad muttered, though his eyes were fixed on the juicy goat leg placed in front of Dabasir.

"Well, I know it's true," Dabasir said, taking a large bite of meat. "Because I once saw the world in a different way myself. And my story is about how I finally learned to see things clearly again."

Nearby diners, hearing Dabasir start a story, scooted closer, dragging their rugs to listen. Others joined, bringing their food and forming a semicircle around him. As they ate, they crunched loudly and brushed Tarkad with their meaty bones. He alone had no food. Dabasir didn't offer to share, not even the hard bread that had fallen onto the floor.

The Fall of a Young Man

"The story I'm about to tell," Dabasir began, pausing for another big bite, "is about my early life and how I became a camel trader. Did any of you know that I was once a slave in Syria?"

Gasps of surprise rippled through the group, and Dabasir smiled, pleased with their reaction.

"When I was a young man," he continued, "I worked as a saddle maker, just like my father. I married a good wife, and though I wasn't highly skilled yet, I earned enough for us to live modestly. But I wanted more. I wanted fine things that I couldn't afford. I soon realized that shopkeepers would let me buy on credit, even when I didn't have the money to pay right away.

"Being young and foolish, I didn't understand that a man who spends more than he earns is setting himself up for disaster. I bought fine clothes, luxuries for my wife, and things for our home—things beyond our means. I paid little by little, and for a while, everything seemed fine. But eventually, I realized my wages weren't enough to cover both our living expenses and my debts.

"My creditors began demanding payment, and life became miserable. I borrowed from my friends, but I couldn't pay them back either. Things got worse. My wife left me and returned to her father. I decided to leave Babylon and seek my fortune elsewhere.

"For two years, I wandered, working for caravan traders, but I never got ahead. Then I fell in with a group of desert robbers who raided unguarded caravans. It was shameful for the son of my father, but I didn't see my own downfall—I was looking at the world through a false lens.

"Our first raid was successful. We stole gold, silks, and treasures. We took it all to Ginir and wasted it in foolish pleasures.

"But our second raid was a disaster. We were ambushed by the guards of a powerful chief. Our leaders were killed, and the rest of us were captured. We were stripped of everything and sold as slaves in Damascus.

The Harsh Reality of Slavery

"I was bought for two pieces of silver by a Syrian desert chief. My hair was shaved, and I was given nothing but a loincloth. I was no different from the other slaves. At first, I thought it was just another adventure—until my master took me before his four wives and told them they could make me a eunuch.

"That was when I truly understood my hopeless situation. These desert men were fierce and powerful. I had no weapons, no way to escape.

"The four women looked me over. I wondered if any of them would have mercy on me. The first wife, Sira, was older. Her face was unreadable, offering no comfort. The second was a beautiful woman who looked at me like I was nothing more than a bug. The two younger ones giggled, as if it were all a game.

"They took their time deciding my fate. Finally, Sira spoke coldly: 'We have enough eunuchs. What we lack are good camel tenders. Even today, I need someone to take me to visit my sick mother, but none of our slaves are trustworthy. Ask this one if he knows how to handle a camel.'

"My master turned to me and asked, 'What do you know about camels?'"

Trying not to show how eager he was, I answered, "I can make camels kneel, load them properly, and lead them on long journeys without tiring. If needed, I can also repair their gear."

"The slave speaks confidently," my master observed. "If you wish, Sira, take this man as your camel tender."

And so, I was given to Sira. That very day, I led her camel on a long journey to visit her sick mother. Along the way, I took the chance to thank her for choosing me. I also told her that I was not born a slave—I was the son of a free man, an honorable saddle maker from Babylon. I shared much of my story with her, but her response troubled me.

A Choice Between Freedom and Slavery

"How can you call yourself a free man," she asked, "when your own weakness has brought you to this? If a man has the soul of a slave, won't he become one no matter what his birth, just as water always finds its level? But if a man has the soul of a free man, won't he still rise to respect and honor in his own city, no matter what misfortunes he faces?"

For over a year, I was a slave and lived among other slaves, but I could not become like them.

One evening, Sira asked me, "Why do you sit alone in your tent when the other slaves gather and enjoy each other's company?"

I answered, "I've been thinking about what you said. I wonder if I truly have the soul of a free man. I cannot join them, so I must sit apart."

"I, too, must sit apart," she confided. "My dowry was large, so my husband married me for it. But he does not desire me. And what every woman longs for is to be desired. Because of this—and because I have no children—I must sit apart. If I were a man, I would rather die than live as a slave, but the customs of our tribe make slaves of women."

"What do you think of me now?" I asked her suddenly. "Do I have the soul of a free man or the soul of a slave?"

"Do you truly want to repay the debts you owe in Babylon?" she asked in return.

"Yes, I do," I admitted. "But I see no way."

"If you let the years pass without trying to repay, then you have only the weak soul of a slave. No man can respect himself if he does not repay what he owes."

"But what can I do?" I asked, frustrated. "I am a slave in Syria!"

"Then stay a slave in Syria, you weakling."

"I am not a weakling!" I protested angrily.

"Then prove it."

"How?"

"Does your great king not fight his enemies in every way he can, using every strength he has? Your debts are your enemies. They chased you out of Babylon. Instead of fighting them like a man, you ran away, and they grew too strong for you. If you had faced them, you could have conquered them and been honored among your people. But instead, you let your pride fall so low that you became a slave in Syria."

The Escape and the Struggle for Survival

I thought deeply about her harsh words. I wanted to defend myself, to prove her wrong, but I didn't get the chance.

Three days later, Sira's maid brought me to her.

"My mother is sick again," Sira said. "Saddle the two best camels in my husband's herd. Tie on water skins and saddle bags for a long journey. The maid will give you food from the kitchen tent."

I did as she asked, but I wondered why the maid packed so many supplies when Sira's mother lived less than a day's journey away.

We traveled, the maid following behind on the second

camel. When we reached her mother's house at nightfall, Sira dismissed the maid and turned to me.

"Dabasir," she asked, "do you have the soul of a free man or the soul of a slave?"

"The soul of a free man," I answered firmly.

"Then prove it. Your master has drunk deeply, and his chiefs are in a drunken stupor. Take these camels and escape. Here in this bag is clothing from your master's household to disguise yourself. I will tell them you stole the camels and ran away while I was visiting my sick mother."

"You have the soul of a queen," I told her. "I only wish I could lead you to happiness."

"Happiness," she said sadly, "does not wait for a runaway wife among strangers in a far land. Go now, and may the gods of the desert protect you. The way ahead is long and empty of food or water."

I needed no further urging. I thanked her deeply and rode off into the night.

I did not know this land, and I had only a rough idea of which direction led to Babylon. But I pressed forward across the desert toward the distant hills. One camel I rode, the other I led.

All that night and the next day, I traveled, knowing the terrible fate that awaited slaves who stole from their masters.

By late afternoon, I reached rough country. The jagged rocks hurt my camels' feet, forcing them to walk slowly. The land was empty. No man or beast dared to live there.

From that moment on, my journey became one that few men survive. Day after day, I pressed forward. My food and water ran out. The desert sun was merciless. By the ninth day, I was too weak to climb back onto my camel. I collapsed to the ground, certain I would die in this wasteland.

When I woke at dawn, I sat up and looked around. The cool morning air touched my skin. My camels lay nearby, exhausted. There was no sign of water, no food—nothing but endless sand and thorns.

Was this the end?

Then, as I stared into the empty distance, a thought came to me.

"Do I have the soul of a slave or the soul of a free man?"

If I had the soul of a slave, I would accept my fate and die here in the desert. But if I had the soul of a free man? Then I would find my way back to Babylon. I would repay my debts. I would bring happiness to my wife. I would bring honor to my parents.

A Determined Man Finds a Way

Sira had been right. My debts had been my enemies, and I had run from them. But why? Why had I not stood my ground like a man?

Suddenly, the world seemed different, as if I had been looking through a colored stone that had now been lifted away. At last, I saw clearly.

Die in the desert? Never!

With new resolve, I made my plan. I would return to Babylon and face every man I owed. I would tell them I had come back to pay, as the gods allowed. I would build a home for my wife and restore my honor.

Weak as I was, I forced myself to stand. Hunger and thirst didn't matter anymore. My camels, sensing my renewed strength, struggled to their feet as well. I pointed them north, toward Babylon.

We found water. We entered a land with grass and fruit. We found the road to Babylon because a free man sees life as a set of problems to solve, while a slave says, "What can I do? I am only a slave."

The Lesson for Tarkad—and for All Men

Dabasir turned to Tarkad. "And you? Does your empty stomach make your mind clear? Are you ready to take the road back to self-respect? Can you see the world as it truly is? Do you have the desire to pay your debts and once again be a man of honor in Babylon?"

Tears welled in Tarkad's eyes. He rose to his knees. "You have shown me a vision. Already, I feel the soul of a free man rising within me."

"And what happened when you returned?" someone asked.

"Where there is determination, a way can be found," Dabasir replied. "I found my way. I asked my creditors for patience, and many were kind. One man—Mathon, the gold lender—helped me find work with a camel trader. Bit by bit, I repaid every debt. At last, I could hold my head high as an honorable man."

Dabasir smiled and turned back to his food. "Kauskor, you slow lizard! Bring fresh meat—and bring a large portion for Tarkad, the son of my old friend. Tonight, he eats with me!"

So ended the tale of Dabasir, the camel trader of old Babylon.

He had lost himself in weakness and debt, but he found his true soul when he realized a great truth—a truth known by wise men long before him.

This truth has helped many escape hardship and find success. It will keep doing so for those who recognize its power.

Where there is determination, a way can be found.

Key Takeaways

1 **A Man's Choices Shape His Destiny.** Dabasir's downfall was not due to bad luck, but his own poor financial decisions. People who spend more than they can afford and avoid responsibility will face trouble eventually.

2 **Debt is a Burden That Must Be Faced.** Running from financial obligations only makes matters worse. Dabasir found that true freedom comes from paying off debts and restoring honor, not from escaping responsibility.

3 **Mindset Determines Success or Failure.** Sira's words

challenged Dabasir to decide whether he had the soul of a free man or a slave. A person who accepts defeat is a slave to their situation. But someone who fights to overcome challenges earns respect and success.

4 Where There is Determination, a Way Can Be Found. Even when Dabasir was near death in the desert, his renewed resolve led him to survival and eventual success. Hardships can be overcome with perseverance and a clear goal.

5 A Free Man Sees Solutions, Not Excuses. Dabasir's story shows that blaming bad luck keeps people stuck. But, taking action—even when it's hard—can help regain dignity and create a better future.

11

THE CLAY TABLETS FROM BABYLON

St. Swithin's College

Nottingham University Newark-on-Trent Nottingham
Professor Franklin Caldwell, Care of British Scientific Expedition, Hillah, Mesopotamia.

October 21, 1934.

Dear Professor,

The five clay tablets from your recent excavation in
Babylon arrived on the same boat as your letter. I'm really
fascinated by them. I've spent many fun hours translating
their inscriptions. I meant to reply sooner but wanted to
finish the translations first. I have attached them to this
letter.

The tablets arrived safe and sound. This is due to your great packing and careful use of preservatives.

You will be just as surprised as we were in the laboratory by the story they tell. Ancient writings often bring to mind tales of romance and adventure, much like those in Arabian Nights. Instead, these tablets reveal the struggles of a man named Dabasir, who was determined to pay off his debts. It makes you realize that, despite five thousand years, some problems in life have barely changed.

It's funny—these old inscriptions really "get to me," as the students say. As a college professor, I am supposed to be a knowledgeable man, familiar with many subjects. Here comes an ancient Babylonian, speaking from the past. He offers a way to get out of debt and even save some gold. It's something I never imagined!

It's an interesting idea. I'm eager to see if his plan will work as well in today's world as it did in ancient Babylon. Mrs. Shrewsbury and I plan to try it ourselves. Our finances could definitely use some improvement.

Wishing you success in your important work. I look forward to helping again. I remain,

Yours sincerely, Alfred H. Shrewsbury, Department of Archaeology

Tablet No. I

When the moon becomes full, I, Dabasir, recently freed from slavery in Syria, set this record in clay. It will serve as my guide as I work to pay my debts and become a respected and prosperous man in my home city of Babylon.

My friend Mathon, the moneylender, gave me wise advice. He said I can follow a plan to help any honorable man get out of debt and find financial security.

This plan has three key parts, which I consider my hope for the future:

1 The plan ensures my future prosperity.

○ I will set aside one-tenth of everything I earn for myself to keep.

○ Mathon says wisely: *"A man who keeps both gold and silver in his purse is good to his family and loyal to his king. A man who has only a few coppers is indifferent to his family and his king. A man with nothing in his purse becomes bitter, unkind to his family, and disloyal to his king."*

○ If I want to succeed, I must have money in my purse—not just for spending, but to keep. That way, I will have love for my family and loyalty to my king.

2 The plan ensures I can support my wife.

○ My good wife, who has returned to me with loyalty, deserves to be provided for.

○ Mathon says that taking good care of one's wife brings self-respect and strengthens a man's purpose.

○ I will use seven-tenths of my earnings for our home, clothing, food, and a little extra for pleasure.

○ However, I must be very careful never to spend more than seven-tenths of what I earn.

○ This is the key to success—I must learn to live within this portion and never spend beyond my means.

Tablet No. II

3 The plan ensures that I will repay my debts.

   ○ Every time the moon is full, I will take two-tenths of what I earn and divide it fairly among those who have trusted me and to whom I owe money.

   ○ In time, this will allow me to pay off all my debts.

Therefore, I now record the names of those I owe and the amounts:

- Fahru, the cloth weaver – 2 silver, 6 copper
- Sinjar, the couch maker – 1 silver
- Ahmar, my friend – 3 silver, 1 copper
- Zankar, my friend – 4 silver, 7 copper
- Askamir, my friend – 1 silver, 3 copper
- Harinsir, the jewel maker – 6 silver, 2 copper
- Diarbeker, my father's friend – 4 silver, 1 copper
- Alkahad, the house owner – 14 silver
- Mathon, the moneylender – 9 silver
- Birejik, the farmer – 1 silver, 7 copper

(From this point, the tablet is damaged and unreadable.)

Tablet No. III

I owe a total of 119 pieces of silver and 141 pieces of copper.

I couldn't repay my debts, so I foolishly let my wife go back to her father. I left home and chased quick riches in another city, but I ended up in disaster. I ended up a slave.

Now that Mathon has shown me how to repay my debts in small, steady amounts, I see how foolish I was to run away.

I have visited my creditors and explained that I have no wealth, only my ability to earn. I have promised to use two-tenths of my income to pay them fairly. Most were understanding.

• Ahmar, whom I once called my best friend, insulted me bitterly. I left feeling humiliated.

• Birejik, the farmer, begged me to pay him first, as he was in great need.

• Alkahad, the house owner, was angry and threatened me.

• The others accepted my plan without complaint.

Despite some difficulties, I am now more determined than ever to follow through. I have realized that it is easier to face one's debts than to run from them.

Tablet No. IV

The full moon shines again, and I have worked hard with a clear mind.

• This past month, buying camels for Nebatur, I earned 19 pieces of silver.

• I divided it according to my plan:

○ 1/10 saved for myself

○ 7/10 for living expenses

○ 2/10 to repay debts

After my first payment, my debt was reduced by nearly four silver pieces. I also saved nearly two silver pieces that belonged only to me. My heart feels lighter than it has in a long time.

Tablet No. V

A full year has passed. Today, I have paid off my last debt!

My wife and I celebrate with a great feast. I will never forget my final visits to my creditors:

• Ahmar apologized for his harsh words and asked to be my friend again.

• Alkahad, who once threatened me, now respects me. He said, *"You were once soft clay, easily shaped by anyone. But now you are like bronze—strong and unbreakable. If you ever need silver or gold, come to me."*

My wife looks at me with pride in her eyes. I walk among my friends with my head held high.

The plan has changed my life.

It has freed me from debt and allowed me to keep gold and silver in my purse. I recommend it to anyone who wants to improve their life.

If an ex-slave can pay off his debts and become financially free—why can't any man?

And I am not finished with this plan. I am certain that if I continue to follow it, it will make me rich.

St. Swithin's College
Nottingham University Newark-on-Trent Nottingham
Professor Franklin Caldwell, Care of British Scientific Expedition, Hillah, Mesopotamia.

November 7, 1936.

My dear Professor,

If you dig in Babylon and meet the ghost of Dabasir, an old camel trader, please thank him for us. A few grateful college folks here in England would appreciate it.

You may recall that, a year ago, Mrs. Shrewsbury and I decided to try out his plan for getting out of debt while also saving a little gold. You might have suspected, though we tried to hide it from our friends, that we were in a desperate situation.

We felt ashamed of our old debts for years. We always worried that a shopkeeper might create a scandal. That could force me out of college. We paid and paid—every shilling we could scrape together—but it was barely enough to keep up with the interest. To make matters worse, we were forced to shop only at places that would extend us more credit, even if their prices were higher.

It became a vicious cycle—things only got worse instead of better. We couldn't even move to a cheaper place because we owed rent to our landlord. It felt like there was no way out.

Then, along came your old acquaintance—the camel trader from Babylon—with a plan that promised exactly what we needed. His words stirred us to action. We wrote down a full list of all our debts, and I took it to every person we owed.

I explained that, as things stood, it was simply impossible for me to ever pay them in full. The numbers spoke for themselves. Then, I told them my solution: I would set aside twenty percent of my income each month and divide it fairly among them. At that rate, every debt would be paid off in just over two years. We would pay for everything in cash. This would help them too, as they'd get regular payments.

They were surprisingly reasonable. Our greengrocer, a wise old fellow, put it best and helped convince the others. "If you pay for what you buy *and* pay something toward what you owe, that's already better than you've done for the past three years."

In the end, they all signed an agreement, promising not to trouble us as long as we stuck to the plan.

Then, we set about figuring out how to live on seventy percent of our income. We were determined to keep the extra ten percent just for ourselves—to jingle, as Dabasir put it. The idea of saving real silver, maybe even gold, was too tempting to ignore.

It actually became quite fun, like an adventure. We found ways to adjust our spending. We cut costs here and there but still lived comfortably. We even managed to negotiate a lower rent. We started questioning the price of our favorite brands and were often surprised to find better quality at a lower cost.

There's much more to tell, but to sum it up—once we made the change, it wasn't difficult at all. In fact, we managed quite well and were happier for it. Most of all, it was an enormous relief to finally have control over our finances and not live in constant fear of overdue bills.

Now, about that extra ten percent we were supposed to keep—well, we jingled it for a while. Don't laugh! That was part of the fun. But eventually, we found a better use for it.

We decided to invest it. Every month, before anything else, we put that ten percent into an investment. And that has turned out to be the most satisfying part of this whole transformation. It's comforting to know that our savings are growing steadily. By the time I retire from teaching, it should be a nice, solid sum—enough to support us for the rest of our lives.

And all of this is happening on the same salary I had before! Hard to believe, isn't it? Yet it's completely true. We are paying off our debts and building our investments. At the same time, we manage our daily expenses more easily than before.

Who knew drifting along could be so different from following a financial plan?

By the end of next year, once all our debts are fully paid, we'll have even more to put into savings—plus a little extra to use for travel. And we are determined never again to let our expenses exceed seventy percent of our income.

Now you understand why we wish we could personally thank that old camel trader. His plan saved us from what truly felt like a *hell on earth*.

He understood. He had lived through it himself. That's why he took the time to carve his message into the clay—to help others avoid the suffering he had endured.

Five thousand years later, his words still echo from Babylon's ruins. They remain as true and powerful as when they were first penned.

Yours sincerely, Alfred H. Shrewsbury, Department of Archaeology

Key Takeaways

1 The Principles of Wealth are Timeless. Dabasir's financial plan, written 5,000 years ago, remains relevant today. Debt and financial insecurity are still big issues. But we can solve them by saving, budgeting, and repaying debts.

2 A Simple Plan Can Lead to Financial Freedom. Dabasir's three-part formula changed his life. He saved 10% of his income, lived on 70%, and used 20% to pay off debts. This plan took him from slavery to financial security. The same method worked for Alfred Shrewsbury and his wife in modern times, proving its effectiveness.

3 Debt is Best Faced Head-On, Not Avoided. Running away from financial problems only makes them worse. Dabasir found that admitting his debts helped. He made a plan and paid them off slowly. This earned him his self-respect and the trust of his creditors.

4 Financial Control Brings Peace and Opportunity. When the Shrewsburys began Dabasir's plan, they felt relief, security, and joy in handling their finances. Paying off debts, saving money, and making smart choices relieved their stress. This also helped them grow wealth for the future.

5 Discipline and Commitment Are Essential for Success. No matter if it's ancient Babylon or modern England, sticking to a financial plan helps. Those who make steady and responsible choices will reach prosperity. Wealth is not about luck—it is about applying sound principles consistently over time.

12

THE LUCKIEST MAN IN BABYLON

A Merchant's Burden

At the head of his caravan, riding proudly, was Sharru Nada, the merchant prince of Babylon. He dressed in the finest robes and rode a magnificent Arabian stallion with ease. He looked strong and confident, and no one would have guessed his age—or that he was deeply troubled inside.

The journey from Damascus was long, and the desert was harsh, but these things did not bother him. He had no fear of the fierce Arab tribes who preyed on rich caravans—his guards were swift and well-armed.

But it was the young man riding beside him that weighed on his mind. Hadan Gula was the grandson of Arad Gula, Sharru Nada's old business partner. Sharru owed Arad a debt of gratitude he could never repay. He invited the young man to Babylon. He hoped to help him start fresh and escape the ruin his father caused their family's fortune.

Yet, the more Sharru Nada considered how to help him, the more difficult it seemed. He glanced at Hadan Gula's flashy rings and earrings. *He thinks jewels are for men,* he thought. *But at least he has his grandfather's strong features. Still, his grandfather never wore such extravagant robes. I brought him here to give him a chance, but how can I help a boy who does not want to help himself?*

A Young Man's View of Wealth

As if reading his thoughts, Hadan Gula suddenly asked, "Why do you work so hard? You're always traveling with your caravans on these long journeys. Don't you ever take time to enjoy life?"

Sharru Nada smiled. "Enjoy life?" he repeated. "And how would you enjoy life if you were me?"

"If I had your wealth, I would live like a prince. I would never ride across this hot desert. I would spend my shekels as fast as they filled my purse. I would wear the finest robes and the rarest jewels. *That* would be a life worth living."

Both men laughed.

"Your grandfather wore no jewels," Sharru Nada remarked before he could stop himself. Then, in a lighter tone, he added, "Would you leave no time for work?"

"Work is for slaves," Hadan Gula scoffed.

Sharru Nada bit his lip but said nothing. He rode in

silence until they reached a slope. Then, he reined in his horse and pointed ahead.

"Look," he said. "There is the valley. If you look closely, you can see the walls of Babylon in the distance. The tall tower is the Temple of Bel, and if your eyes are sharp, you might even see the smoke from the eternal fire burning at its peak."

"So that is Babylon?" Hadan Gula said eagerly. "I have always wanted to see the richest city in the world. My grandfather built his fortune there. If only he were still alive, we would not be struggling as we are now."

A Debt of Gratitude

"Why wish for his spirit to remain on earth longer than it was meant to?" Sharru Nada asked. "You and your father should carry on his good work."

"Alas," Hadan Gula sighed, "neither of us has his gift. We do not know his secret for attracting golden shekels."

Sharru Nada did not reply. He gave his horse a light kick, and they rode on in thoughtful silence. Behind them, their caravan followed, raising a cloud of reddish dust.

While traveling on the King's Highway near Babylon, Sharru Nada noticed three old men plowing a field in the lush, irrigated farms. There was something strangely familiar about them.

How ridiculous, he thought. *One does not pass a field after forty years and find the same men still plowing it.* And yet, something deep inside him told him they were indeed the same men.

One of them struggled to hold the plow steady, his grip uncertain. The other two walked beside the oxen, half-heartedly striking them with wooden staves to keep them moving.

Forty years ago, he had envied these men.

He had longed to trade places with them. But now, looking back at his caravan, filled with fine goods from Damascus, he saw how much had changed. *What a difference time makes.*

Pointing to the plowers, he said, "Still plowing the same field they were in forty years ago."

"They *look* like they could be the same men," Hadan Gula admitted, "but how can you be sure?"

"I remember them," Sharru Nada said simply.

Memories rushed through his mind. *Why can't I just bury the past and live in the present?* But then, he saw a familiar face in his mind—the warm, smiling face of Arad Gula. The barrier between himself and the arrogant young man beside him seemed to fade.

But how could he truly help Hadan Gula? The boy was spoiled, wasteful, and had no interest in hard work. Sharru Nada could offer work—plenty of it—but not to a man who thought himself too good for it. And yet, he owed it to Arad Gula to try. Not a half-hearted attempt. He and Arad Gula had never done things that way.

A Difficult Lesson

Suddenly, an idea came to him. It would be difficult. It would be cruel. It would hurt. But it was the only way.

Being a man of quick decisions, he pushed aside his doubts and chose to act.

"Hadan Gula," he said, "would you like to hear how your worthy grandfather and I became business partners?"

"Why not just tell me how you made your fortune?" Hadan Gula said lazily. "That's all I need to know."

Sharru Nada ignored the remark and continued.

"We start with those men plowing the field. I was no older than you when I first saw them. I was part of a group of men marching past, and Megiddo, a farmer who was chained beside me, scoffed at their lazy plowing. 'Look at those fools,' he said. 'The man holding the plow barely tries to cut deep, and the beaters do not even keep the oxen in line. How do they expect to grow good crops with such poor work?'"

A Shocking Revelation

Hadan Gula frowned. "Did you say Megiddo was *chained* to you?"

"Yes, with bronze collars around our necks and a heavy chain linking us together," Sharru Nada said. "Next to him was Zabado, a sheep thief I had known in Harroun. At the end of the chain was a man we called Pirate because he refused to tell us his real name. He had serpent tattoos on his chest, which made us think he was a sailor. The whole column was chained together in rows of four."

"You mean—you were a *slave*?" Hadan Gula asked in shock.

"Did your grandfather never tell you that I was once a slave?"

"He often spoke of you," Hadan Gula admitted, "but he never hinted at that."

"He was a man you could trust with your deepest secrets," Sharru Nada said. He looked Hadan Gula in the eye. "Are *you* such a man? Can I trust you?"

"You have my word," Hadan Gula said seriously. "But I am still amazed. How did you become a slave?"

Sharru Nada shrugged. "Any man can find himself a slave. For me, it was gambling and barley beer that led to disaster. My brother got into a fight and killed a man. To save him from the law, my father gave me as a bond-servant to the dead man's widow. But when he failed to raise the silver to buy back my freedom, she became angry and sold me to a slave dealer."

A Slave's Fate

"What a terrible injustice!" Hadan Gula exclaimed. "But tell me—how did you regain your freedom?"

"We will get to that," Sharru Nada said, "but not yet. Let me continue."

"As we passed, the plowers mocked us. One of them even took off his ragged hat, bowed low, and called out, 'Welcome to Babylon, guests of the King! He awaits you on the city walls, where your banquet of mud bricks and onion soup is prepared!'

"The others laughed loudly.

"This enraged Pirate, who cursed them all.

"Confused, I asked him, 'What do they mean by saying the King awaits us?'

"Pirate spat on the ground. 'They mean we're going to be worked to death carrying bricks up the city walls,' he growled. 'But they won't beat *me* to death—I'll kill them first.'"

Work: A Curse or a Salvation?

"Then Megiddo spoke up. 'It doesn't make sense for a master to beat a hardworking slave to death,' he said. 'Masters like good workers. They treat them well.'"

"Who wants to work hard?" scoffed Zabado. "Those plowmen are smart. They're not breaking their backs, just pretending to work."

"You can't get ahead by being lazy," Megiddo argued. "If you plow a full field, that's a good day's work, and any master knows it. But if you only plow half, that's slacking off. I don't slack off. I like to work, and I take pride in doing a good job. Work has been my best friend—it gave me everything I had: my farm, my cows, my crops, everything."

"Oh yeah?" Zabado sneered. "And where are all those things now? I say it's better to be clever and get by without working. Just wait and see. If we get sold to the wall builders,

I'll end up carrying the water bag or doing some easy task. Meanwhile, you, who love to work, will be breaking your back hauling bricks." He let out a foolish laugh.

A Desperate Plea

That night, terror gripped me. I couldn't sleep. I crept close to the guard rope and, when the others were asleep, I caught the attention of Godoso, one of the night guards. He was one of those ruthless Arab bandits—the kind who, if they stole your purse, would think they ought to cut your throat, too.

"Godoso," I whispered, "when we get to Babylon, will we be sold to the wall builders?"

"Why do you ask?" he said cautiously.

"Can't you understand?" I pleaded. "I'm young. I want to live. I don't want to be worked or beaten to death. Is there any chance I could get a good master instead?"

He whispered back, "Listen carefully. You're a good fellow —you don't cause trouble. Most of the time, we go to the slave market first. When buyers come, tell them you're a hard worker. Make them *want* to buy you. If no one buys you, tomorrow you'll be carrying bricks. That work is miserable."

After he walked away, I lay in the warm sand, staring up at the stars, thinking about work.

Was Megiddo right? Could work really be a friend? Could it save me?

When Megiddo woke up, I whispered my good news to him. It was our one small hope as we marched toward Babylon.

A Glimpse of Horror

Late that afternoon, we reached the city walls and saw lines of men climbing up and down steep paths, like black ants. As we approached, we noticed thousands of workers. Some dug trenches, others mixed clay for bricks. Most carried heavy baskets of bricks up the steep slopes.

Overseers screamed at them, cracking whips over their backs.

I saw exhausted men collapse under their loads. If they couldn't get up, they were dragged to the side and left there, groaning in agony. Others lay motionless, waiting for their unmarked graves.

I shuddered.

So this is what awaited me if I failed at the slave market.

Godoso was right.

We were taken through the city gates to a slave prison, and the next morning, we were herded into holding pens at the market. The others were terrified, moving only when the guards whipped them.

But Megiddo and I spoke eagerly to every buyer who would listen.

The slave dealer brought in soldiers from the King's Guard, who shackled Pirate and beat him brutally when he protested. As they led him away, I felt sorry for him.

Megiddo, sensing that we might soon be separated, spoke to me one last time.

"Some men hate work. They make it their enemy. But work is a friend—it makes you strong, it builds character.

Think about the good things you are creating, and don't worry if it is hard. If you build a house, does it matter if the beams are heavy? If you mix plaster, does it matter if the well is far? Promise me this: if you get a master, work for him as hard as you can. Even if he does not appreciate it, never mind. Work will make you a better man."

An Unexpected Opportunity

Just then, a burly farmer came to examine us.

Megiddo immediately started asking about his farm and crops. Soon, he had convinced the farmer that he was the perfect worker. After intense bargaining, the farmer pulled a fat purse from beneath his robe, and just like that, Megiddo was led away to his new home.

One by one, other men were sold.

By noon, Godoso told me the dealer was getting frustrated. He planned to sell all the remaining slaves to the King's brickworks at sundown.

I was desperate.

Just then, a fat, kind-looking man approached the pens.

"Is there a baker among you?" he called out.

This was my chance.

I stepped forward and said, "Why should a great baker like yourself settle for an average one? Wouldn't it be better to train a hardworking man like me in your skilled ways? Look at me—I'm young, strong, and I love to work. Give me a chance, and I will make gold and silver for your purse."

The baker was impressed. He began bargaining with the

slave dealer—who, until then, had barely noticed me. Suddenly, the dealer raved about my skills, my good health, my cheerful nature.

Finally, the deal was struck.

I followed my new master away, thinking I was the luckiest man in Babylon.

A New Beginning

My new home was pleasant. My master, Nana-Naid, was a good baker. He taught me how to grind barley, build the oven fire, and grind sesame flour for honey cakes.

I had a bed in the grain shed, and the old slave housekeeper, Swasti, fed me well. She liked how I helped her with heavy tasks.

This was my chance to make myself valuable and, hopefully, earn my freedom.

I asked Nana-Naid to teach me how to knead dough and bake bread. He was pleased with my enthusiasm.

Later, I asked him to show me how to make honey cakes, and soon, I was doing *all* the baking.

Nana-Naid was delighted—he became lazy, leaving everything to me.

But Swasti shook her head.

"No work to do is bad for any man," she muttered.

I began to think—how could I start earning coins for myself?

Since our baking was done by noon, I had free afternoons. If Nana-Naid allowed it, I could find extra work and share my earnings with him.

Then, an idea struck me—why not bake extra honey cakes and sell them in the streets?

I pitched my idea to Nana-Naid.

"If I use my afternoons to make us extra money, would it be fair for you to share the profits with me? Then I could save a little for myself, to buy the things every man desires."

He agreed.

"Fair enough, fair enough," he said. When I explained my plan to sell honey cakes, he was pleased.

"We'll do it like this," he suggested. "Sell them at two for a penny. Half of the earnings will cover the cost of flour, honey, and wood. The rest—we split."

I was thrilled—I would get one-fourth of my sales!

The First Step Toward Freedom

That night, I built a tray to carry the cakes. Nana-Naid gave me an old robe, and Swasti patched and washed it for me.

The next day, I set out with my tray, calling out my wares.

At first, no one was interested. I felt discouraged.

But as the afternoon wore on and men grew hungry, they began buying. Soon, my tray was empty.

Nana-Naid was pleased, and paid me my share.

I held my first pennies in my hand—my own money.

Megiddo had been right. A master appreciates a hardworking slave.

That night, I could hardly sleep. I imagined how much I

could earn in a year, how many years it would take to buy my freedom.

And so, my journey truly began.

A Cruel Reminder

I often went outside the city gates to sell my goods to the overseers of the slaves who were building the walls. I hated seeing such terrible sights, but the overseers were good customers. One day, I was shocked to see Zabado waiting in line to fill his basket with bricks. He looked thin and weak, his back covered in welts and sores from the overseers' whips. I felt sorry for him and handed him a cake. He crushed it into his mouth like a starving animal. When I saw the hunger in his eyes, I ran away before he could grab my tray.

The Value of Hard Work

"Why do you work so hard?" Arad Gula asked me one day. It was almost the same question you asked me today—do you remember? I told him what Megiddo had said about work, how it was proving to be my best friend. I proudly showed him my small wallet of coins and explained that I was saving to buy my freedom.

"When you are free, what will you do?" he asked.

"Then," I said, "I will become a merchant."

At that, he confided in me something I had never

suspected. "You don't know this, but I, too, am a slave. I am in business with my master."

Hadan Gula's Outrage

"Stop," Hadan Gula interrupted angrily. "I won't listen to lies that insult my grandfather! He was never a slave!" His eyes burned with rage.

Sharru Nada remained calm. "I honor him for rising above his misfortune and becoming a respected man in Damascus. But are you, his grandson, strong enough to face the truth? Or would you rather believe in comforting lies?"

Hadan Gula straightened in his saddle. His voice trembled with emotion as he replied, "My grandfather was loved by all. He did countless good deeds. When famine struck, wasn't it his gold that bought grain from Egypt? Didn't his caravans bring food to Damascus so that no one would starve? And now you say he was just a despised slave in Babylon?"

"If he had remained a slave in Babylon, then yes, he might have been despised," Sharru Nada answered. "But through his own efforts, he became a great man in Damascus. The gods forgave his past misfortunes and honored him with success."

A Life-Changing Decision

Sharru Nada continued, "After telling me he was a slave, Arad Gula explained how desperate he was to buy his freedom. But now that he had saved enough money, he was unsure what to do. His sales had slowed, and he was afraid to leave the security of his master's protection.

"I scolded him for his hesitation. 'Don't cling to your master any longer. Regain the feeling of being a free man! Act like a free man, and you will succeed like one! Decide what you want to achieve, and work will help you reach it!' He left, saying he was glad I had shamed him for his fear.

"One day, I went outside the gates again and saw a huge crowd gathering. When I asked what was happening, a man replied, 'Haven't you heard? An escaped slave killed one of the King's guards. He has been caught and will be flogged to death today. Even the King himself will be there to watch.'

The Fate of Pirate

"The crowd around the flogging post was so dense that I was afraid of spilling my tray of honey cakes. So I climbed up the unfinished wall to see over the people's heads. From there, I was lucky enough to catch a glimpse of King Nebuchadnezzar himself as he rode by in his golden chariot. I had never seen such luxury—his robes and the decorations of his chariot shone with gold and velvet.

"I couldn't see the flogging, but I could hear the poor slave's screams. I wondered how such a noble-looking King could endure such cruelty. But when I saw him laughing and joking with his nobles, I knew he was heartless. I finally understood why the slaves who built his walls suffered so much.

"After the slave died, his body was hung from a pole by a rope tied to his leg so that everyone could see. As the crowd thinned, I moved closer. On his hairy chest, I saw a tattoo—two entwined serpents. It was Pirate.

Arad Gula's Transformation

"The next time I met Arad Gula, he was a changed man. He greeted me with excitement. 'Look! The slave you once knew is now a free man! There was magic in your words. My sales and profits are already increasing. My wife is overjoyed! She was a free woman, the niece of my master. She wants us to move to a new city where no one will know I was once a slave. That way, our children will never suffer because of my past. Work has become my greatest ally—it has given me back my confidence and my skill in selling.'

"I was overjoyed that I had helped him in even a small way, just as he had once encouraged me.

A Sudden Misfortune

(*Slavery in ancient Babylon, though it may seem strange to us, was strictly regulated by law. For example, a slave could own property, even other slaves, and his master had no claim to it. Slaves often married free people, and their children were considered free. Many merchants were slaves. Some formed business partnerships with their masters. This helped them become wealthy on their own.*)

"One evening, Swasti came to me, deeply troubled. 'Your master is in trouble,' she said. 'I fear for him.

"Some months ago, he lost a lot of money gambling. He hasn't paid the farmers for their grain or honey. He hasn't paid the moneylender either. They are angry and threaten him.'

"'Why should we worry about his foolishness?' I replied carelessly. 'We are not his keepers.'

"'Foolish boy, you don't understand,' she said. 'To get a loan, he gave the moneylender your ownership papers as security. By law, the moneylender can claim you and sell you. I don't know what to do! He is a good master. Why should such misfortune come upon him?'

"Swasti's fears were not unfounded. The next morning, while I was baking, the moneylender arrived with a man named Sasi. Sasi looked me over and said I would do.

"The moneylender didn't even wait for my master to return. He simply told Swasti to inform him that I had been taken. With only the robe on my back and the small purse of coins tied safely to my belt, I was forced away from my work.

Back to Slavery

"It felt like all my hopes had been ripped away, as if a storm had torn a tree from the forest and thrown it into a raging sea. Once again, gambling and barley beer had brought disaster upon me.

"Sasi was a rough, harsh man. As he led me across the city, I told him about my good work for Nana-naid and my hope to be useful to him. His response was far from encouraging:

"'I don't like this work. My master doesn't like it either. But the King ordered him to send workers to build a section of the Grand Canal. My master tells me to buy more slaves, work them hard, and finish quickly. Bah! How can any man finish a big job quickly?'

"Imagine a desert with no trees, just small shrubs, and a sun so hot that the water in our barrels became too warm to drink. Picture rows of men digging deep into the earth, hauling heavy baskets of dirt up steep, dusty paths from sunrise to sunset. Our food was dumped into open troughs, and we ate like animals. There were no tents, no beds—just the hard ground to sleep on. That was my new life. I buried my small wallet of coins in a marked spot, wondering if I would ever dig it up again.

Doubt and Reflection

"At first, I worked hard, but as the months dragged on, my spirit began to break. The heat fever weakened me. I lost my appetite and could barely eat the tough mutton and vegetables. At night, I lay awake, restless and miserable.

"In my suffering, I wondered if Zabado had been right to avoid work and protect his back. But then I remembered how broken he had looked, and I knew his way was not good.

"I thought of Pirate, who had chosen to fight and kill. But the memory of his lifeless body reminded me that his way was also wrong.

"Then I remembered Megiddo. His hands were rough from labor, but his heart was light. His face was filled with happiness. His way was the best way."

Yet, I was just as willing to work as Megiddo. He couldn't have worked harder than I did. So why didn't my work bring me happiness and success? Did work truly make Megiddo happy, or were happiness and success simply left to the will of the gods? Would I work my whole life and never achieve my dreams? Would I never find happiness or success? These questions filled my mind, but I had no answers. I was deeply confused.

Summoned Back to Babylon

Several days later, just when I felt I could endure no more and my questions remained unanswered, Sasi sent for me. A messenger had arrived from my master, calling me back to Babylon. I dug up my precious wallet, wrapped myself in the torn remains of my robe, and left.

As we rode, my feverish mind was filled with thoughts of being tossed around like a leaf in a hurricane. It reminded me of an old chant from my hometown of Harroun:

It strikes a man like a whirlwind, Drives him like a storm, No one can predict its path, No one can foresee its end.

Was I doomed to be tossed around by fate forever, punished for reasons I didn't understand? What new struggles and disappointments awaited me?

A Life-Changing Reunion

When we arrived at my master's house, I was shocked to see Arad Gula waiting for me. He helped me down from my horse and embraced me like a long-lost brother.

As we walked together, I instinctively followed him the way a slave follows his master, but he wouldn't allow it. Instead, he put his arm around my shoulder and said, "I searched everywhere for you. Just when I was about to lose hope, I found Swasti. She told me about the moneylender, who then led me to your noble owner. He drove a hard bargain and made me pay an outrageous price—but you are worth it.

"Your wisdom and determination have inspired me to reach this new level of success."

"It was Megiddo's wisdom, not mine," I said.

"Megiddo's and yours," he replied. "Thanks to both of you, we are going to Damascus, and I need you as my partner. Look!" He pulled a clay tablet from beneath his robe. "In just a moment, you will be a free man!"

He lifted the tablet—my ownership record—above his head and smashed it onto the ground. It shattered into a hundred pieces on the cobblestones. Laughing with joy, he stomped on the broken fragments until they were nothing but dust.

Tears of gratitude filled my eyes. I knew I was the luckiest man in Babylon.

The True Power of Work

"You see," I said, "work has proven to be my greatest friend, even in my darkest hour. My willingness to work saved me from being sold into the gangs of slaves building the walls. It also impressed your grandfather so much that he chose me as his partner."

Hadan Gula thought for a moment and then asked, "Was work my grandfather's secret to gaining wealth?"

"It was the only key he had when I first met him," Sharru Nada replied. "Your grandfather enjoyed working. The gods saw his efforts and rewarded him well."

"I'm beginning to understand," Hadan Gula said thoughtfully. "Work brought him many friends who admired his determination and success. Work earned him the honors he loved so much in Damascus. Work gave him everything that I have always been proud of. And yet, I used to think work was only for slaves."

"Life offers many pleasures for men to enjoy," Sharru Nada said. "Each has its place. But I am grateful that work is not reserved only for slaves. If it were, I would be deprived of my greatest joy. I enjoy many things in life, but nothing fulfills me like work."

A Humble Decision

Sharru Nada and Hadan Gula rode through the towering walls of Babylon toward its massive bronze gates. As they approached, the guards stood straight and saluted an honored citizen. With his head held high, Sharru Nada led the long caravan through the gates and into the streets of the city.

"I have always hoped to be like my grandfather," Hadan Gula admitted. "But until now, I never truly understood what kind of man he was. You have shown me that. Now that I know the truth, I admire him even more—and I am determined to follow in his footsteps. I don't know how I can ever repay you for revealing the true key to his success. From this day forward, I will use his key. I will start humbly, as he did, because that suits my true place far better than jewels and fine robes."

With that, Hadan Gula removed the jeweled ornaments from his ears and the rings from his fingers. Then, with a deep sense of respect, he pulled back his reins and fell behind, riding humbly behind the leader of the caravan.

Key Takeaways

1 **Hard Work is the Key to Success.** Sharru Nada and Arad Gula both began with nothing. Still, they built amazing fortunes. Their success came from hard work, dedication, and persistence. Wealth is not inherited or magically acquired—it is earned.

2 **Work is a Friend, Not a Curse.** Some people, like Hadan Gula, view work as a burden. But others, like Megiddo and Sharru Nada, embrace it. They find that work

brings fulfillment, stability, and prosperity. Work builds character and earns respect.

3 Fortune Favors Those Who Take Control of Their Destiny. Sharru Nada could have stayed a helpless slave. Instead, he seized every chance to better his situation. He learned new skills and looked for business chances. He showed his worth, which helped him gain freedom and wealth.

4 A Life of Luxury Without Purpose is Empty. Hadan Gula thought wealth was all about fancy clothes and jewels. Hearing Sharru Nada's story opened his eyes. He knew that real wealth comes from meaningful work, strong relationships, and helping the community.

5 Every Man Chooses His Path. Some, like Zabado, take the path of laziness and end up suffering. Others, like Pirate, choose rebellion and meet a tragic end. Those who embrace hard work and persistence, like Arad Gula and Sharru Nada, overcome their struggles. They achieve lasting success.

EPILOGUE

Babylon's wisdom endures for a good reason. Financial success relies on discipline and wise choices. It's about taking control of your money, not just luck or privilege. The lessons in this book have helped many people build wealth, escape debt, and create financial security. They can help you too.

The principles are simple: Save at least a portion of what you earn. Invest wisely. Protect your wealth. Avoid risky ventures. Seek knowledge and advice from those with experience. These truths worked for the Babylonians thousands of years ago, and they still work today.

But knowledge alone isn't enough. The key to financial success is action. Begin today. Save your first ten percent. Pay off debts. Learn about investing. Small, consistent steps will lead to lasting prosperity.

Wealth is built, not wished for. Security is earned, not

given. And success is within reach for anyone willing to follow these timeless laws of money.

Now, it's up to you. What will you do with this knowledge?

This wraps up the modern version of The Richest Man in Babylon. It's a classic guide for growing wealth, making wise financial choices, and ensuring your future.

But financial wisdom doesn't stop here. This book is part of the For Everyone series, a collection of timeless works rewritten in clear, modern language. We bring history's key ideas to you. Now, you can learn from great thinkers without battling through heavy, old texts.

The For Everyone series covers philosophy, personal growth, and financial success. This knowledge has helped leaders, thinkers, and everyday people for centuries.

If you found this book helpful, be sure to explore the rest of the series. Each book makes profound insights easy to understand and apply.

Thank you for reading, and remember—wealth is built not by luck, but by learning and applying the right principles. The wisdom of the past is just as valuable today, and your journey to financial freedom continues."

www.ingramcontent.com/pod-product-compliance
Lightning Source LLC
Chambersburg PA
CBHW071720140626
46557CB00012B/979